THE DECEPTION OF MATERIALISTIC WESTERN PHILOSOPHY

By Julian Hamer

© All rights reserved. No part of this publication may be reproduced without the prior permission of the author.
First published, 2015

Dedicated to my beautiful wife Ellen

THE DECEPTION OF MATERIALISTIC WESTERN PHILOSOPHY
An Exploration of the Physically Elusive, Immanent Volume of Existence

By Julian Hamer

Contents

     Introduction
1. Inherent Significance p5
2. Abstract Philosophy p11
3. Physical Ambiguity p15
4. Immanence p19
5. Immediate Cognition p25
6. Essential Ipseity p29
7. Human Individual Distinction p35
8. Essential Circumstances p41
9. Conscience p47
10. Intangible Volume p51
11. Materialistic Myopia p55
12. The Petty Sense-of-Self p59
13. Definitive Knowledge p63
14. Acumen and Scholarship p67
15. Value and Consequence p71
16. The Temper of the Soul p75
17. Transilience p79
18. Assumed Foreknowledge p85
19. Beyond Physical Coordinates p89
20. Human Essential Distinction p93
21. The Original Encounter p97
22. The Transformative Event p101
23. Immediacy p105
24. Open-Mindedness p109
25. Oblique Thinking p113
26. Receptivity p117
27. Theory and Speculation p121
28. The Essential View p125
29. Caprice p129
30. Caritas p133
     Books by the same author p137

Introduction

The existence of a human, incorporeal distinction is denied by an inveterate, materialistic Western philosophy. Through the eyes of materialism, the individual is considered to be entirely corporeally composed and particular identification is solely attributed to the idiosyncratic singularity of the organism.

However, the denial of the existence of an essential, intangible ipseity has enormous repercussions upon human wellbeing and hinders the realization of a meaningful destiny because thereby we remain ignorant of our authentic identification.

The significance of the human, essential identity rests upon its elemental nature. From the perspective of the individual, unique principle, the similarly essential condition of all other phenomena is discovered. If its existence is categorically denied then the efficacy of immediate cognition is rendered moot.

The human, essential ipseity is vastly more significant than the physical constitution through the permanence and innate identity possessed by an entity that is absent from an organism. Ipseity exists both elusively and immanently, and it is unrestricted by physical coordinates.

Through the disavowal of intrinsic significance and the allocation of identity solely to human corporeality, we surrender our inherent capacity to directly engage circumstances and to discover their absolute condition. Thus, cognition remains oblique and we must rely upon rationale, influenced by our particular convictions and affections. Consequently, the absolute status of phenomena becomes equivocal through the inevitable partiality of vagrant and digressive thinking.

Furthermore, exclusive materialism compounds the human plight in an even more insidious manner. It abstractly conceives and depicts existence in simplistic, tangibly obvious terms that contradict even empirically derived intelligence. Through the entirely physical nature of the permissible information, an inevitably mechanistic interpretation of existence is established that represents a mere carapace of reality.

This banal assessment of life further impedes human maturation because it burdens the soul with apprehension. A sense of meaningless and insignificance that is not easily dislodged augments an inherent suspicion of inadequacy that arises through the conviction that the petty sense-of-self is our authentic identification.

This profound malaise remains untouched by conventional psychology particularly if the practitioners themselves are ignorant and ambiguous concerning the human, essential constitution. The antidote does not rest with rationale or behavior modification but with the experiential discovery of the human, essential principle.

But the human, moribund soul cannot self-ameliorate because that would require a dual identification. Our own attempts towards self-amendment merely lead to Puritanism and self-righteousness. We cannot know the nature of an emancipated and sovereign constitution, or we would already have relinquished the petty sense-of-self and identified with a nobler mentality.

However, the reparation of this impasse is readily accessible to us. Through openhearted sincerity, the human soul renders itself vulnerable to the corrective of immanent caritas that is implicit and immediate within the meaningful volume of existence. Thereby, the installation of a new archetypal paradigm is inaugurated through its own direct influence within the foundation of the individual constitution.

1. Inherent Significance

*The **Quality** is that which is inherent in the thing and coexistent; the **Property** is that which belongs to it for the time being; the **Attribute** is the quality that is assigned to any object. We cannot alter the quality of a thing without altering the whole thing; but we may give or take away properties from bodies at pleasure, without entirely destroying their identity; and we may ascribe attributes at discretion.*
All introductory quotes are from George Crabb (1778 – 1851) English Synonyms

Intrinsic value is only indirectly dependent upon the physical conditions of its appearance in much the same way that the content of a book is of greater significance than the ink, the pages and the binding. Entrenched materialistic, Western philosophy has come to consider the exterior to be of greater significance than the essential consequence because intangible merit exists elusively and its existence cannot be physically justified.

Physically elusive existence is incomprehensible from a philosophical point-of-view that is established exclusively upon evidence derived from the phenomenal aspects of things. Within the obvious appearance, the materialist struggles to find essential meaning where none exists and searches for a conceptual architecture that will explain existence within the confines of material parameters. The palpable conditions and properties are scrutinized in molecular detail. But all that is recovered is information concerning the physical particulars and their workings which, upon extrapolation inevitably present a mechanical interpretation of existence. Meanwhile, the essential identification remains remote since it cannot be materially isolated because it does not exist tangibly but intrinsically.

No one denies the existence of the qualitative value of things, but we have managed to contrive a philosophy that purports to explain existence merely upon the basis of the superficial composition. By disregarding the intangible proportion of phenomena, we arrive at a conceptual artifice that reduces existence to sterility and irrelevance because significance does not reside solely within the physical composition.

Nevertheless, intrinsic connotation resides imperceptibly as a qualitative elaboration of the physical. Therefore, materialism is a superficial rationalization that does not resemble the entirety but resides notionally, in the human imagination. But material exclusivity has become the dominant philosophical perspective whereby the shallow appearance of things has taken precedence over the inherent significance.

When we pursue the doctrine of materialistic, Western philosophy to its logical implication, we find only impoverishment because everything that is of essential but intangible significance will be discounted as extraneous. However, the inherent value of something exists elusively, and existence inevitably becomes meaningless when we merely consider the transient periphery as if it were the entirety of a phenomenon. We imagine that the corporeal prospect of something can endure without the elusive connotation of essential distinction and qualitative particularity, but it cannot because it is with the intangible significance of a thing that the authentic identification and subsequent relevance lies.

Disregard for the physically elusive pertinence of phenomena reduces them in our perception to mere shadows of their comprehensive significance. Physical analysis may reveal that two similar items possess identical properties but scrutiny solely of the physical conditions cannot reveal the qualitative singularity. However, upon the intangible distinction rests the essential particularity and differentiation between them.

The inability of physical examination to reveal the qualitative dimension of something is the legerdemain most common to the food industry. Technical methodology is used to advantage to conceal the intangible distinction between similar crops. Hence, a genetically modified, synthetically grown vegetable is compared to sun-ripened organic produce and pronounced to be identical. This is only possible because qualitative distinctions are elusive to physical analysis.

When we investigate the physical properties of something separately from the meaningful volume, we fail to grasp the significance of the whole. In order to discover what something really is, all factors including the intangible, qualitative attributes must be included otherwise we will assume that a partial representation constitutes the entirety.

If we attempt to extrapolate the information that we have gleaned from an exhaustive examination of the physical representation, inevitably we arrive at an inconsequential conclusion because we have mistakenly assumed that the physical appearance of something is exclusively substantial. Examining the blatant, tangible and aggregated attributes of things is fruitless in the search for the unified distinction because it is the essential status that determines identity. Hence, the material condition of phenomena cannot exist in separation from their qualitative and intrinsic integrity and retain meaning because significance resides intangibly and not merely physically.

The transitory, physical conditions of something are restricted within the parameters of duration and location while the intrinsic essence remains independent of chronology and amplitude. Thus, that which exists elusively, such as the content of a book or the substance of a work of fine art, is of vastly greater significance than the appearance even though it is sensibly impalpable. The magnitude wherein intrinsic essence resides is immanent in the sense that it is not dependent on physical circumstances. Within the infinity of its extension, all significance is to be found and, for that reason, the corporeal status of things is justly regarded as the superficial countenance.

The essential identification of the human being similarly resides within an immanent, incorporeal context. However, through an insidious deception, we have become convinced that the transient and mutable body describes our particular distinction. In the same manner whereby we overlook the essential significance of other things because the intrinsic connotation is impalpable, we regard our own identification in physical and transitory terms. Thereby, our habitual thinking practices are materially circumscribed and consequently, intangible, immanent existence inevitably remains an unfathomable concept.

Whether we understand the concept of an intangible, immanent, dimension to existence is beside the point because unless immanence is directly experienced it remains merely a hypothetical concept however convincing the contention. There is, nevertheless, an essential element of the human constitution that exists intangibly and is capable of discovering the validity of elemental existence through direct, experiential cognition. Thus, every person possesses the capability of discovering the meaningful volume of things for themselves through the immediate engagement of the human, essential ipseity.

The intrinsic identification of the human being is able to recognize itself through unequivocal experience and subsequently discerns the essential, singular uniqueness of all other people and the implicit distinction of phenomena. Through immediate engagement we encounter phenomena without interpretative distortion. We find that the human, essential ipseity exists immanently as our own meaningful volume and significance. Within the same condition of immanence, the intrinsic identification of all other things similarly reside.

2. Abstract Philosophy

*A person is said to be abstracted...or follow an abstracted theory when the mind is altogether abstracted from external or sensible object; a thing is said to be **Abstract** which is formed by the operation of abstraction or abstract thinking, as an abstract idea which is abstracted or separated by the mind from the object to which they belong and inhere; whiteness is an abstract idea, because it is conceived in the mind abstracted from snow, a wall, or any other substance that is white.*

The inevitable tendency of the materialist is to explore for meaning primarily within the obvious composition of things because the intangible relevance of something is inaccessible to physical identification. However, the value, quality and essential of phenomena possess intrinsic significance that is not found within the structure alone. In fact, the formation of something, isolated and estranged from the intangible volume, is inevitably deprived of all meaning and connotation.

Material conditions are unequivocal and easy to substantiate but intangible value seems ambiguous because it must be experientially ascertained. However, that does not mean that intangible subtleties do not exist or that intrinsic nuances, implicit coloring and qualitative distinction are of only marginal relevance. Yet, it is upon exclusively palpable evidence that the abstract theory of materialistic, Western philosophy is established.

Tendentious, abstractly conceived ontologies that are exclusively predisposed towards a selective caliber of evidence, have wreaked havoc upon civilization in the past and continue to threaten human advancement. Intolerance, dogmatism and pedantry were once considered the domain of an oppressive religious pedagogy. However, materialistic, Western philosophy has become similarly, insidiously entrenched. As of old, the majority remain in ignorance while existential knowledge seemingly remains the sole prerogative of a scholarly and scientific elite who claim to possess the crucial acumen and understanding.

Through an exclusive emphasis upon information derived from the material properties of things, the physically elusive value and meaningfulness of existence is depreciated and, consequently, we imagine ourselves as merely corporeal and all phenomena as correspondingly mundane. Conceivably, this myopia might remedy itself over time like any other erroneous conviction that is eventually found to be unworkable in practice. But the renunciation of the intangible essence of the human constitution has grave repercussions because it is through the aegis of the singular distinction that objective experience and definitive, existential knowledge is attainable.

Conventionally, physically elusive conditions are considered recognizable only through sensible association which is necessarily idiosyncratic and, consequently, the qualitative value of something can only be substantiated through consensus. Furthermore, the meaningful volume of a phenomenon cannot be described in physically relevant terms because it exists without the necessity of tangible properties. But it must be expressed descriptively and figuratively because it is only indirectly coincident with matter and, accordingly, it remains unquantifiable.

But we each possess a constitutional resource whereby we can identify the intangible, meaningful volume of things both experientially and conclusively. Direct cognition is accomplished through an immediate engagement between the human, essential identification and phenomenal circumstances. Thereby the inherent distinction of people and of things becomes evident because the human ipseity resides in an essential consonance with the intrinsic significance of everything.

The consequences of an excessive identification with corporeality and the assumption of a materialistic philosophy that refutes the existence of essential ipseity, disable human maturation towards cognitive autonomy. However, we only contradict the essential significance of things abstractly through contrived reasoning. In practice, we experience intangible significances constantly, and metaphorically, the fine artist is able to articulate those conditions through an appropriately expressive medium.

An enduring conflict remains between the human, direct experience of the reality of intangible subtleties and significances and an abstractly conceived interpretation of existence that is established upon a doctrine of material exclusivity. Furthermore, materialism is supported by scientific methodology. But science deals precisely, only with tangible existence and, consequently, the resort to subjective evaluation in order to qualify physically elusive information, is disparaged. Thus, restrictive attention to the physical status of things reduces our perception of existence to a mere shell of what actually exists because essential merit does not reside within exclusively material conditions.

In reality, the results of the scientifically disciplined inquiry are not as objective nor as encompassing as its adherents would have us believe. This is particularly the case when materially dependent information is stretched to establish a philosophical interpretation of existence because it excludes physically elusive significances that are indispensable to a sound understanding.

Unlike temporal, physical conditions, essential existence is consistent. That is, meaningful proportion of things lies solely within the enduring volume of their inherent singularity. Thus, material conditions without intangible content would appear arid and superficial because they are detached from their significance.

As distinct from material analysis, immediate cognition from the viewpoint of the human, essential ipseity does not engage apparent circumstances but discovers the absolute existence of things through direct encounter. Thereby it discerns the antecedent identification of phenomena because through its own emphatic condition of existence, it recognizes similarly elemental particularities. It finds things as they exist intrinsically and originally without the embellishment of human conjecture and presupposition.

The engagement of circumstances through the immediate experience of the perspective of essential ipseity, through its directness reveals to us the definitive distinction of things. Therefore, it is objective in absolute terms. Explicit cognition of this nature delivers conclusive knowledge because it enables us to identify the innate, existential consequence and significance that otherwise lies beyond conventional, preoccupied perception.

3. Physical Ambiguity

***Tangible** is used figuratively to denote anything that may be readily grasped by the mind and proved to exist; in this sense we speak of tangible reason, of tangible evidence , etc. Real...is applied to those things which have actual existence. Where the proof of existence is thought to be demonstrable by the sense, real means having a physical form.*

The essential, human being cannot directly enter into the tangible realm except through the agency of the biological vehicle. The physical body belongs amidst all other tangible phenomena. But the architecture of the essential human constitution demonstrates a materially elusive magnitude that is of the same disposition as a concept of human invention that exists physically only when realized through manufacture.

From childhood, we must steadily develop the proficiency and competence that is required in order that we may successfully govern our corporeal circumstances and thereby we become capable of effective interaction within the Earth environment. But when we excessively identify with the phenomenal appearance of things and assume that our own identification corresponds with our tangible status, we obstruct an essential overview and existence loses all meaning and pertinence for us. Subsequently, we assume that we share the plight and limitation of the animal because we circumscribe our comprehension within the materialistically established parameters that we see.

The physically constricted view of our own

identification spawns an exclusively materialistic interpretation of existence that obstructs and delays the accomplishment of our incarnate objective of existential maturation. Materialistic myopia effectively impedes our progress because it disables the realization and positioning of the human, essential ipseity as our sovereign autonomy. With the entrenched conviction of an exclusively physical existence, henceforth, we reject the human essential condition that alone assures our liberation.

Emancipation from a materialistically circumscribed mentality that obscures the meaningful volume of existence, rests upon the recognition of the significance of human, essential individuality. But we are additionally constricted by the cumulative acquisition of a moribund disposition that is established upon the confusion that originates from corporeal preoccupation. Furthermore, absorption with our physical segregation precipitates a conviction of self-circumscription and subsequent apprehension for our continuance that in extreme circumstances appears as egomania. We imagine that our intrinsic identification is correspondingly corporeally limited and indistinguishable from the body.

Through immediate cognition, we find that the intrinsic significance of things occupies the same volume wherein resides the human, essential ipseity. But habitually we fail to directly engage circumstances and consider them only in the abstract or through subjective appraisal. Consequently, the isolated, material condition of phenomena, void of meaning and volume, appears to represent the totality of existence and our perspective remains merely superficial.

This is particularly apparent in terms of human relationships. If we imagine that the distinctiveness of another person is limited to their corporeality, we will associate with them in an accordingly superficial manner. But when the impalpable, intrinsic significance is recognized as their authentic identification, we meet them both profoundly and considerately because we determine the individual entity itself who is otherwise physically elusive. We find that we can do them no harm because through the establishment of immediate concurrence, it would seem to us as if we misused something sacred. We find that the essential ipseity of another exists in a condition of immediacy with that of our own elemental uniqueness.

In order to discover the inherent distinction of a person or of a thing, we must approach them from the viewpoint of our essential ipseity. Thus, we discover the intrinsic pertinence of a phenomenon or the unique particularity of another person because we engage them not spatially but essentially. We effectuate a correspondence that exceeds the material circumstances, and we thereby engage the full volume that epitomizes their existence.

The tangible portion of things is that which is recognizable through physical means. It does not include quality or value, intrinsic distinction or essential significance. All these things reside intangibly in an immanent continuum of existence that is immediately accessible to the human, essential ipseity. The essential meaningfulness of something is of vastly greater significance than the appearance because the intangible volume is both consequential and constant. Therefore, immediate engagement from the viewpoint of the human, essential singularity reveals the complete circumstances of its particular existence.

The elemental distinction of something cannot be determined from merely physical evidence, but it must be experientially encountered. Reduction and quantification only apply to the degree whereby the properties of something may be measured and calibrated but physical analysis cannot discern the essential value of something because mensuration does not address meaning and significance. While the implication of intrinsic consequence may be suggested through the scrutiny of material circumstances, essential existence cannot be conclusively identified on the strength of the physical testimony alone. Blatant material conditions are incongruous in relationship to essential particularities because the essence of something remains untouched by physical scrutiny.

When we view existence only in terms of material appearances, we diminish phenomena merely to their ostensible, spurious aspects. The resultant depiction is inevitably void of all the qualities that give life meaning and purpose because pertinence and intention are tangibly elusive values. The inclusion of our own identification within a superficial evaluation of existence, inevitably hamstrings further development because it invalidates the human, essential ipseity. However, the unique, individual distinction can be immediately engaged and from that perspective we may recognize the full volume and meaning of existence and thereby attain authentically independent understanding.

4. Immanence

*The **Superficial** is that which lies only at the surface; it is therefore by implication the same as the shallow, which has nothing underneath...Superficiality is applied to the exercise of the thinking faculty and shallowness to its extent. Superficial and shallow are applicable to things as well as persons...In the improper sense, a survey or a glance may be superficial which does not extend beyond the superficies of things.*

Materialistic, Western philosophy contradicts our immediate experience because it excludes physically elusive information concerning existence and fabricates a one-side interpretation that endeavors to explain phenomena solely in tangible terms. Although we recognize and constantly contend with knowledge derived from impalpable circumstances, our intellectual understanding of existence is strongly biased towards the tangible.

It is easy to be certain concerning the readily perceivable appearance of things but their qualitative value and particular, intrinsic distinction requires an altogether different experiential approach. Thus, we discover a contradiction because material existence is obvious while the essential meaningfulness of something is predominantly found within the elusive volume of existence that is physically unapparent.

The essential, qualitative distinction of a phenomenon is only inconsistently assessed through conventional cognition because it cannot be decisively identified through subjective experience.

For example, a description and the interpretative representation of the nature of the color red, may differ significantly from the depiction of the same color by another person however impartial each may strive to be. Through the essential inconsistency of experiential cognition and the difficulty of definitive identification, the physically elusive dimension of phenomena, where value and meaning reside, is excluded from our philosophical assessment of life. Subjectively derived information is subsequently interpreted in physical terms through analytical reduction and quantification to whatever degree possible, however slight that may be. Physically elusive information that doggedly lingers but is physically remote and imperceptible, is dismissed as an idiosyncratic anomaly of the mind and the senses.

While the experiential perception of a phenomenon may vary through the idiosyncratic nature of the human, physical constitution, astuteness and perspicacity significantly reduce the impact of the discrepancy. However, in order that intangible significances may be described and accurately communicated, a suitable medium of expression must be mastered.

Art is the metaphoric language where with the essential conditions of things are represented. If a particular, artistic skill remains uncultivated and inadequately developed, it is less the inconsistency of the elusive incident that is at fault and more the inadequacy of the narrator.

The proper identification of something must include the elusive, intangible proportion otherwise it is only an incomplete assessment established upon the obvious, physical properties. Conversely, if subjective cognition is entirely without physical representation, it is similarly incoherent.

Immediate cognition fundamentally differs from subjective evaluation because the direct engagement of the human, essential ipseity eliminates the need of interpretation. Ipseity does not evaluate but approaches circumstances emphatically without rationale or partiality and thereby discovers the actual identification of something. Both the human, essential ipseity and the intrinsic distinction of the object exist in a relationship of immanence with one another. Immanence is where the essential and meaningful volume of existence, overlooked by materialistic, Western philosophy, resides.

Materialistically motivated philosophy presents an intellectual explanation of life that endeavors to decipher everything in physical terms. Thereby a rationalized structure is established that is composed solely of the results of physical scrutiny. It is tenuously maintained in the face of commonsense by convoluted, conceptual justification that endeavors to force everything into compliance. Materialistic, Western philosophy is a skillfully contrived ontology that has become entrenched within the human psyche as an inhibited frame of reference that distorts comprehensive discernment.

We are ignorant of immanent continuance because our understanding has become spatially restricted and the notion of an immediate existence that possesses essential significance seems all but the stuff of make-believe. But when we realize that all that is of profound value and meaningfulness exists beyond the blatant physical appearance of things, our perspective is expanded. Without the inclusion of intangible merit, our perception of life presents merely an arid and purposeless semblance of that which we know empirically through even the most mundane activities and experiences.

Furthermore, when we consider the qualitative value of a thing, we must wonder where it resides if it is not materially apparent and if it escapes physical evaluation. If reduction, analysis and quantification presents a true depiction of an elusive quality then that same representation must similarly reveal the original value that it claims to exemplify.

For example, two fruits may be refined into their chemical constituents but strict analysis, nevertheless, fails to reveal the qualitative distinction between artificially grown produce that is tasteless and sun-ripened organic food that is both flavorsome and nourishing.

Through immediate cognition we objectively discover the inherent value and distinction of things and recognize that we are able to discern the intrinsic condition of something because the human, essential ipseity is similarly, incorporeally authentic. Without a direct experience of immanent existence, we continue to imagine a solely spatial existence and endeavor to explain intangible significances superficially within the parameters of physical limitation. Thus, artificial concepts arise of rarefied existence or parallel universes that attempt to compensate for the physical absence of an essential origin and motivation for phenomenal appearance.

The identification of the particular, intrinsic

distinction of a person or thing, is accomplished through an immediate concurrence between the person or phenomenon, and the human, essential ipseity. It is only the physical that exists spatially. The meaningful volume of existence is directly and experientially encountered and found to occupy a condition of immanence.

The consequence of materialistic, Western philosophy is a barren mechanistic interpretation of existence. Materialism is a deception that only recognizes physical circumstances and attempts to reduce and explain everything intangible through material connotation. Thereby, existence is robbed of essential value and meaning. But we recognize the forced nature of materialism through our own experience of physically elusive value. Furthermore, we possess the capacity to know the full status of existence and thereby directly discover its authentic circumstances. That capability resides inherently with our own singular and intrinsic identification and therein lies our cognitive liberation.

5. Immediate Cognition

Substantial *beings are such as consist of flesh and blood, and may be touched, in distinction to those which are airy or spiritual...So in the moral (conceivable in the imagination) application, the substantial is opposed to that which exists in the mind only and which is frequently fictitious.*

The manner in which we may discover the intrinsic nature of existence and experience it instantaneously, requires the restraint of conventional perception and assessment. It is necessary to inhibit all presumption and accumulated acumen in order that we can engage circumstances originally and ascertain the actual state of things before we tarnish our impressions with indiscriminate evaluation. In other words, preference, partiality and bias merely obstruct direct cognition, and they must be tempered in order that we may engage things unpolluted by human, habitual distortion.

We wish to reestablish the original and unaffected manner of an encounter that we briefly practiced in early childhood before we established a discriminatory, interpretative slant towards existence. Direct cognition is made possible by arresting our customary, rationale and affected estimation of things and thereby straightforwardly engaging circumstances and finding their authentic condition.

Existence is of a certain nature and complexion and it does not change merely because we discover its actual disposition. It is we ourselves who have established a jaundiced viewpoint towards life and consequently we garner the unfortunate consequences of a disparate perspective because we assume things to be other than they are. If our knowledge of existence is ambiguously established and further intensified through penchant and partiality, we construct for ourselves a fanciful context upon which basis our relationship towards existence is decided.

Each person interprets life according to a certain predilection. But existence itself is not altered one iota by our particular stance or preference. We may be convinced of a certain interpretation of circumstances but whatever we imagine and assure ourselves concerning the nature of things, does not impact reality but merely distorts our judgment.

We render a presumptive image of life according to accumulated perception and assessment but we do not influence its actual status anymore than we can claim to have engineered existence itself through our convictions. The real caste of things is far beyond our interference and control. There is only one reality and if we misinterpret its features, inevitably our relationship towards things will be distorted and our subsequent dealings will be incongruous. Therefore, it is imperative that we accommodate the authentic nature of existence in our minds, otherwise we adopt a substitution of our own making that is at variance with the way things really are.

However, to grasp an exposition of existence conceptually but without specific experience, constitutes not knowledge but belief and conviction. This is of no especial advantage to us because it is the same approach that, in our ignorance, we already favor and indulge.

Through the immediate, cognitive engagement of a phenomenon, without the interference of presumption and partiality, we discover the particular quality and texture of its nature. This is the authentic appellation of a thing because through our direct approach, we encounter the essential condition of its existence.

The direct, experiential apprehension of something inevitably establishes a different viewpoint than conventional perception because without the predisposition of intellection, association and affection, the human ipseity is at liberty to squarely engage. Thus, the human, unique distinction becomes positioned as the sole, cognitive perspective towards circumstances and thereby discovers the legitimate condition of their essential status.

Immediate cognition from the viewpoint of the human, essential ipseity, provides direct knowledge of the real nature of things and delivers us a lodestar whereby we recognize the authentic tenor of existence through qualitative comparison. Henceforth, regardless of philosophy or religious conviction, nothing less will satisfy because we have glimpsed reality and we know of its disposition and timbre.

Thus, we inaugurate an entirely straightforward approach towards life because we are determined to engage circumstances on their own terms and not according to humanly contrived assumption. We permit existence to be whatever it may be and, through receptivity, we immanently encounter the unperceived meaningful volume of the existence of things.

6. Essential Ipseity

***Empirical**...refers to knowledge gained simply from observation and experience... A **Hypothesis** is the formulation of a possible law which has not yet been fully demonstrated by experience...That which is experimental may be as yet unformulated; that which is hypothetical may be formulated, but not yet proved by experiment. **Provisional**...means taken as truth or right until a better way can be discovered; it is a formulation of a principle or method of action with the distinct expectation that it will be superseded; and it is intended to serve as a means to an end.*

Materialism is an abstract dogma that discounts the intangible significances of phenomena because they are elusive to purely physical investigation. However, the staunch rationalist does not regard physicalism as a belief but considers it irrefutable because the obvious appearance of things is readily discernible and demonstrable while intangible value is incommensurate with the corporeal.

The flawed premise of materialistic, Western philosophy is its physical exclusivity. It is established upon the assumption that nothing except material conditions possesses actual significance because intangible existence cannot be sensibly verified. It is a contrived ideology that denies intangible existence because its inclusion is unmanageable in physical terms and consequently, inconvenient to appraise.

The quality of a phenomenon such as that of the native-element-mineral silver, is essential and not physical. Quality is specific and while it influences the physical properties of hardness, weight, color and chemical propensity, the quality itself is physically elusive.

There are many more intangible significances that exist beyond doubt but remain excluded from the materialistic credo and consequently render it an inadequate philosophy. For example, the intrinsic distinction of something is its authentic identification and of more profound weight than the idiosyncratic properties but it too is disregarded because it is physically unapparent. Similarly, conceptual origin is invisible and obscure when we examine a manufactured item but no one supposes for a moment that the object was made and assembled by chance circumstances.

When intangible significances are openly included as the crucial and compelling substance of life, the excesses of materialistic, Western philosophy will be moderated. It will become evident that the physical aspects and properties of things are solely applicable to apparent circumstances and through the partiality of materialism, they are an entirely inadequate approach and basis for a philosophy of existence.

Not everything is physical and a philosophy that excludes intangible existence, overestimates its reach and appears as nonsense in the light of empirically derived understanding. It attempts to force an abstractly conceived doctrine upon incommensurate circumstances by dismissing their merit through incompatibility.

Materialism is an insidious indoctrination because it rejects the meaningful volume of things. It reduces all phenomena, including the human being, to a mere carapace of their authentic existence. While the materialist will tacitly acquiesce to the reality of a greater dimension of significance than solely the physical because such things as quality and value cannot be conveniently denied, it will not influence the materially exclusive stance one iota. Furthermore, the location of the intangible volume of things as immanently extant, raises considerable ire and indignation because dimension is only understood in exclusively physical terms.

Materialistic, Western philosophy has become an entrenched mindset towards existence that distorts our entire existential correspondence. It is not commonly realized how meaningful and necessary the recognition of the intangible volume of phenomena is to a correct apprehension of life. It is thought that the quality of something is merely parenthetical to the material status. In reality the reverse is the case because the intrinsic significance of things rests not upon the superficial properties but resides essentially. The elemental distinction of something is its authentic identification although it remains physically obscure and cannot be described in the same terms as tangible circumstances. Intangible significances are physically indiscernible but nonetheless they are discovered as undeniably extant through immediate cognition.

The rejection of data upon the grounds of its elusive physicality naturally adds support to a materialistically exclusive philosophy and accordingly makes it increasingly inaccessible to challenge. Thus, materialism is recognized as a contrived device of self-deception because it is maintained by conviction and not through empirical exploration. Otherwise, the subtle existence of the intangible qualities of phenomena would be carefully evaluated and appropriately included.

If something is subjectively identified, even though it cannot be physically substantiated it does not necessarily follow that it does not exist. The apprehension of the materialist derives from a cognitive ambiguity between physical certainty and an experientially ascertained, elusive existence that cannot be definitively authenticated in the same physical manner.

The materialist is both ignorant and anxious of the practice and implication of immediate cognition, imagining that knowledge concerning intangible existence is only subjectively and capriciously ascertained. The fear is that questionable knowledge established upon physically elusive conditions is the province of a select few and such insight that is offered must be accepted on faith. But immediate cognition is the common aptitude of all human kind because we each possess essential ipseity. It is materialistic, Western philosophy that has established an elite scholarship that is the sole domain of the learned and it is the rest of us who are required to accept materialistic dogma on faith.

The concept of immediate cognition rests upon the experiential recognition of the human, essential ipseity without which it is meaningless. Essential ipseity is intangible and only recognizes itself through immediate encounter in the same direct way that the physically elusive volume of all phenomena is discovered. But materialistic, Western philosophy effectively prohibits expansion because it relies upon a limited cognitive approach that can never accept the intrusion of an extant, intangible volume to existence. Deductive rationale is similarly inadequate to the task and thus the materialist is moribund within an ambiguous limbo that cannot be effectively reconciled unless abstractly contrived, materialistic exclusivity is relinquished to candid empiricism.

Through the incommensurate nature of exclusively physical inquiry with that which is discovered directly through experiential observation, the materialist inevitably remains ignorant of the intrinsic constitution of the human being. Essential ipseity is self-ascertained and subsequently established as the viewpoint from which the similarly intrinsic distinction of all other things is discovered. But materialistic circumscription inevitably denies its existence.

The human, essential ipseity does not require refinement or transformation because it is fundamentally established, However, our corporeal circumstances place entirely different demands upon us. Unfamiliar with the human, essential significance, it appears to us that our physical predicament comprises the entirety of our existence and this ignorance inspires apprehension.

Recognized through immediate cognition as a continuum, human existence is no longer perceived as a transitory progression of episodes and events but our essential ipseity is found to continue unceasingly and emphatically. Thus, we find ourselves secure within the instant, while events, including our physical mortality, continue to transpire about us.

The deception of the material exclusivity of existence is revealed through the practice of immediate cognition because thereby we discover the intransient and elemental volume of things. Consequently, it becomes evident that a narrow perspective hinders straightforward understanding. However, aware of the human, intrinsic identity through direct, experiential observation and alert to the continence of the human, essential ipseity, we begin to establish an opposite rapport with life from the tunnel vision of materialism.

7. Human, Individual Distinction

__Conceptions__ are either grand or mean, gross or sublime; either clear or indistinct, crude or distinct; __Notions__ are either true or false, just or absurd. The unenlightened express their gross and crude conceptions of a Superior Being by some material and visible object; the vulgar notion of ghosts and spirits is not entirely banished from the most cultivated parts of any country.

Failure to distinguish and acknowledge the essential significance of others and to recognize a parity of importance and relevance between them and ourselves, is an anathema because it contradicts the fundamental reality of mutually endowed distinction. It is the madness of self-circumscription whereby we assume that our personal consequence is greater than that of another. Moreover, the posture of self-importance obstructs the recognition of the human, essential condition and condemns us to apprehensive isolation.

The phrase *The Survival of the Fittest,* coined by Herbert Spencer (1820 – 1903) is usually applied out of its hypothetical context. When the concept is adapted as the accepted countenance of human behavior, it provokes an entirely regressive mentality. It is an approach that enhances self-circumscription and thereby perpetuates and preserves egotism and insularity which is counter to the human, essential nature. It is a conceit that when applied in human affairs, reduces us to the status of the animal and we inevitably share a similarly disconsolate plight.

The animal is condemned to remain within the

narrow confines of its characteristic expression, a disposition that is further consolidated through the correlation between its particular physiognomy and habitual temperament. The animalian appearance corresponds to an accumulated disposition that only alters through its dispositional response to ecological challenge. That is why domesticated animals no longer resemble their natural cousins. Through domestication, we alter the aboriginal context of the creature by human association and companionship. Consequently, the animal responds and alters in temperament and, correspondingly, in appearance.

The human being is differently composed than the animal. Within the human constitution resides the potential of existential liberty through the realization and positioning of the essential ipseity as our sovereign identification. While fauna identifies only with the instincts of flock or herd, the human being possesses unique distinction that when realized can eclipse biological predisposition.

No one can see the human, essential ipseity because it is without direct physical correspondence. But from the viewpoint of our intrinsic singularity we are able to recognize the same original distinction in others that we ourselves possess. Thereby we find the essential significance of one another, and we discover that it mirrors our own most profound consequence.

Recognizing the intrinsic distinction of another person has nothing to do with sentimentality. It is of vastly more profound significance because it is achieved only through the viewpoint of our own essential identification. Equating the human being to the creature and maintaining that we possess merely a physically dependent identity, denies the existence of the very thing that distinguishes humanity from the animal and which enables each of us to mature towards essential liberty and autonomy.

The essential significance of people or of things is not biologically obvious, but it exists intangibly as an absolute and elemental identification. Material representation disguises the authentic distinction, and we consequently assume that the physical represents the entirety. In reality, the quintessential statement of the existence of a person or of a thing is not the temporal appearance, but an emphatic, immaterial continuance.

Through direct acquaintance we know that another human being is very inadequately identified on the basis of mere corporeality because we can readily distinguish between a superficial and a meaningful relationship. But we cannot conclusively prove the existence of a physically elusive, essential particularity. Therefore, we endeavor to reconcile the contradiction between experientially derived knowledge concerning the human essence with the necessity of providing convincing confirmation that must be physically demonstrable in order to be satisfactorily authenticated. The materialistic sceptic is ignorant of the significance of immediate cognition and therefore derides experientially obtained information as subjective and effectively negates it.

The dismissal of the existence of a human essential and intangible distinction reveals the abstract nature of materialistic, Western philosophy and the presence of a constricted extremism that categorically denies the value of uncertainty. While we are unable to definitively prove the presence of something that is physically elusive because intangibility is incommensurate with customary sensibility, through impartial experience we discover considerable, supportive evidence.

As young children, we had to come to terms with corporeality and steadily learn how to function in myriad ways within circumstances that were evidently, entirely alien to us. This education is unattainable through the mere reciprocity between biological activity and consequence because it involves imagination, interest and persistence. If we were without an intrinsic, unique significance beyond the physical, then the body itself would inflexibly develop and self-educate. But the respective variation in the particular quality of volition, resoluteness and interest between individuals implies not uniformity but the existence of unique individuality. Thus, we recognize not merely the physical body but an extant entity at work with specific designation and individual determination that is essential to the progressive development of the particular child towards maturity. Through simple, open-minded observation we discern the presence of an innate singularity. This is the human, essential ipseity whose existence is arbitrarily denied through the materialistic partiality of an abstractly conceived philosophy.

The materially exclusive perspective towards life does not correlate with actual experience. It inevitably disregards the significance of physically elusive circumstances and value, and establishes a speculative, irrational condition that determinedly ignores intangible significance. However, direct experience reveals the physically imperceptible, meaningful volume of existence that can only be contradicted at the expense of lucidity and sound judgment.

    Familiar, human correspondence and everyday experience deny the credibility of the philosophy of material exclusivity and reveal it to be a contrived and speculative presupposition. It is maintained in support of the rationale that everything real must be physically authorized or otherwise it is discounted as merely inconclusive knowledge. Thereby, the tangible properties of things are isolated and promoted as an accurate rendition of existence because the elusive proportion of phenomena remains unamenable to physical scrutiny. However, it is merely a hypothetical requirement that maintains that all of existence must fit into physical proportions. In reality, exclusively physical correspondence is not the nature of existence and inevitably conducting ourselves according to a spuriously established, materialistic philosophy reduces human interaction and our approach towards life itself, to mere superficiality.

8. Essential Circumstances

Conjecture, Supposition, Surmise. *All these terms convey an idea of something in the mind independent of the reality...Antiquarians and etymologists deal much in conjectures; they have ample scope afforded them for asserting what can neither be proved nor denied: religionists are pleased to build many suppositions of a doctrinal nature...on their own partial and forced interpretations of the Scriptures: it is the part of prudence, as well as justice, not to express any surmises which we may entertain, either as to the character or conduct of others, which may not redound (contribute) to their credit.*

A systematic and methodical approach towards understanding that conclusively distinguishes between the truth or falsehood of a premise, functions favorably to the degree that it resembles mathematics. Consequently, conducive to calculation, we endeavor to reduce and quantify phenomena into numerical terms and manage them numerically in order to distinguish and identify them accurately by their quantifiable characteristics.

Chemical compounds are represented by formulae that reflect a merger of separate elements with idiosyncratic properties in very specific proportions that, in combination, express an entirely different nature from the features of the individual factors. In this manner, the characteristics of an amalgam of elements including water and air and under the influence of heat and light, is rendered both mensurable and predictable.

But in order to discover the essential significance

that epitomizes and distinguishes a particular Element, it is necessary to proceed beyond the merely idiosyncratic characteristics. Through immediate engagement, the human, essential ipseity encounters the principle of the existence of a phenomenon that is its authentic identification. In the manner whereby we interact with another human being outwardly on the basis of their physicality, personality or temperament, similarly, phenomena may be superficially approached or distinctively identified by their intrinsic uniqueness.

The intangible significance of something is irreducible, unquantifiable and unamenable to calculation because it does not possess quantity and, consequently, it is intractable in physical terms. We recognize the physical repercussions of the elemental distinction of something by its characteristic properties. Thus, the native-element-mineral copper possesses a permanent elusive, distinction of existence that is echoed through its temporal, physical properties but, nevertheless, it remains unrecognizable through its material attributes alone.

If we assume that the physical configuration of a phenomenon is the full extent of its existence, we fail to apprehend it meaningfully and a decisive identification eludes us. Similarly, in human affairs, the appearance of someone does not reveal who they are and should our interaction remain superficial, then an authentic coincidence between the respective human entities cannot occur.

The crux of human emancipation from the peculiar plight of existential estrangement, rests upon the discovery of the essential condition of existence. Our predicament is that we find ourselves through secession preoccupied with the least significant, peripheral condition of things. We assume that the superficial comprises the entirety, and we are unaware of the consequential volume that is concealed by our absorption with exclusively material conditions.

We have constructed entire philosophies that purport to explain existence from a materialistic viewpoint that are completely oblivious to the crucial constitution wherein the significance and meaningfulness of things reside.

A philosophic worldview that is established upon the peripheral circumstances of things, is misleading to humanity because it trivializes existence through the shallowness of its perspective. In the same way as the native-element-mineral copper is assumed by the materialist to be composed entirely of physical characteristics, or another human being is reduced to the status of a biological automaton, the essential merit and meaningfulness of things is overlooked in favor of outward appearances. We may explore the appearance of things with greater precision and alacrity but thereby we merely enter more deeply into the presumption of material exclusivity.

The deception is further compounded as we attempt to classify everything, including physically elusive significances such as value, quality and intrinsic identification, through oblique quantification. Thereby we imagine that we have grasped the essential of something while in fact we depreciate its inherent designation through numerical misrepresentation. The intangible imperative of the existence of something is unamenable to physically dependent classification and to suggest that the calibration of the effect of something represents its intrinsic condition, reveals an ignorance of the elemental significance of things.

For example, the physical consequence of sunlight is measured for its heat and luminosity, and it is further qualitatively classified by the incidence of color through diffusion. The Earth's atmosphere disseminates and diminishes daylight, accordingly, blue, red and a myriad of other colors predominate depending on the particular environmental circumstances, much to the delight of the artist.

But the calibration of these effects does not reveal the intrinsic significance and identification of daylight because mensuration cannot represent the essential existence of a phenomenon but merely gauges the ramifications of its presence. Furthermore, the qualitative capacity of daylight to animate and sustain life is utterly unrepresented through quantification because the essence of invigoration is entirely without physical proportion and it is only identified through direct experience. However, through immediate cognition, we discover something about the intrinsic significance of sunlight that does not correspond with the popular, physical image of a radioactive fireball.

The elusive significance and intrinsic identification of phenomena lose their value entirely through preponderant, physical analysis and scrutiny and thereby our viewpoint remains merely superficial. Through a materialistic myopia, we assume that existence is entirely composed of obvious, material constituents and propelled by reaction. This presents a morbid, mechanistic depiction that is discovered to be remote from reality when circumstances are engaged directly by the human, quintessential designation.

    It is the essential establishment of things that possess relevance because therein lies their authentic identification. Similarly, it is the intrinsic authority of the human being that is able to discern the core identity of others and of phenomena because the essential exists emphatically and not merely corporeally and superficially. Immediate cognition is the practice of experiential engagement that discounts superficial conditions because it recognizes them as merely peripheral. Direct engagement recognizes the intrinsic, elemental essence of existence.

    A legitimate depiction of existence must include both the material condition of things and the physically elusive essential significance. But we fail in the task because we assume that we lack the means to conclusively assess intangible value. Furthermore, the inhibition of a materialistically dominant philosophy hinders the direct experience of the human, essential ipseity that is imperative to immediate cognition. Needless to say, the intangibly extant, human distinction alone is capable of immediate engagement and the decisive identification of the elemental circumstances of things. Without the establishment of the ipseity as the sovereign perspective of the human being, we remain in ignorance of the authentic status of existence.

9. Conscience

***Wonder**...amounts to little more than a pausing of the mind, a suspension of the thinking faculty...**Surprise** and **Astonishment** both arise from that which happens unexpectedly; they are a species of wonder differing in degree, and produced only by the events of life: the surprise, as its derivation implies, takes us unawares.*

Through the restraint of deliberation, abstract conjecture and affective evaluation, we bypass the customary practice of an associative preconception and engage circumstances directly without assumed foreknowledge. We are no longer preoccupied with our own evaluation of the nature of things but discover their relevance as they exist of themselves, independently of our summation.

Immediate, impartial cognition permits us to recognize the intrinsic, emphatic distinction of things because without the inference of presupposition and assumption, our own essential singularity is able to engage circumstances straightforwardly. Furthermore, we become aware of our own significance as the direct observer whereby the human, essential ipseity discovers its own unique existence. We find that we cannot identify our singular individuality merely with our corporeal constitution and, furthermore, we discover that we reside not materially but elusively.

However, lest we deceive ourselves through an overestimation of our own importance, we similarly recognize by direct engagement, the exclusive individuality of everyone else and the essential nature of all things. Heartened by these astonishing discoveries, we further recognize through immediate cognition, the inherent wonder of existence and we become increasingly encouraged and determined in our practice.

But the errant, human heart as the seat of the soul, is another matter entirely because it is not remedied through insight alone. Our dispositional constitution has become disoriented towards self-preeminence and subsequently it imposes upon our progress. We do not possess a duality of soul whereby an enlightened disposition may instruct and amend a mercenary nature. Consequently, we are unable to restore and restructure our own temperamental disposition without engendering an essential conflict of interest.

Moreover, under the advocacy of a healthy conscience, we recognize and loathe our deficiencies and shortcomings but we find that we are unable to effectively modify our disposition without external guidance. Should we strive for goodness through resolution, our attempts to reorder our nature will not transmute our aberrant proclivities but merely reorder them. Thus, of our own efforts, righteousness becomes self-righteousness and purity inclines towards Puritanism because we cannot graft virtue upon a constitution that is inherently oriented towards self-interest.

Conscience reveals the deficiencies and foibles of the human character but we cannot self-ameliorate our unsettled disposition. However, through immediate cognition, we discover the essential amplitude of existence wherein the significance of things resides not spatially nor corporeally but intrinsically. We eagerly encounter the reality of an imminent volume of meaningfulness that was formerly unrecognizable. It is to this magnitude that we turn our hearts in order that our moribund disposition may be reformed. Thereby we directly discover the epitome of integrity that is our own future countenance. We open the soul towards the immanent presence of caritas, not in order to dispel the discomfiture of an active conscience but so that our redundant disposition may be reestablished upon a basis of selflessness and magnanimity.

Contemplation through openhearted sincerity is not synonymous with Eastern meditational practices that provide relief from disquietude through self-induced neutrality. Serenity is obviously beneficial but in terms of the amelioration and reorientation of the human psyche from self-circumscription, permanent resolution only occurs under the aegis of the immanent presence of caritas. Our task is openhearted sincerity and receptivity.

Thus, we recognize the vital importance to our further development of a steady vigilance towards the remonstrations of conscience. To censor qualm and remorse, and endeavor to circumvent their influence works entirely against our own highest interest and hinders the realization of a meaningful, human destiny. Through the acceptance of the insights of conscience and the deliberate willingness of a sincere and open predisposition, transformation of soul through immanent goodwill is inevitable.

The human, moribund disposition of self-circumscription and the attendant proclivity to position foremost our own self-interest, inhibits all our efforts and determination to progress. Unless our resolve is redirected and we permit the entry and influence of supernal caritas into the human soul, we remain moribund. If self-circumscription is not corrected, humanity will unquestionably degenerate towards an animalian state and thereby obstructs further progress towards our destined stature of sovereign liberty.

We must not work against the disagreeable and troublesome challenge of conscience but recognize its value and welcome its corrective influence. It is vital that we accustom ourselves to its reproof and to the restorative aegis of immanent caritas because therein lies our emancipation. The conscience is of imperative importance to the renewal of an insipid frame of mind that has supplanted an essential innocence and incorruptibility that through qualitative transformation will be superseded by maturation and decency.

10. Intangible Volume

*A sky is **Clear** that is divested of clouds: the atmosphere is **Lucid** in the day, but not in the night; the sun shines **Bright** when it is unobstructed by anything in the atmosphere; lightening sometimes presents a **Vivid** redness, and sometimes a vivid paleness: the light of the stars may be clear, and sometimes bright, but never vivid; the light of the sun is rather bright than clear or vivid; the light of the moon is either clear, bright, or vivid. These epithets may with equal propriety be applied to color as well as light: a clear color is unmixed with any other; a bright color has something striking and strong in it; a vivid color something lively and fresh in it.*

The determined materialist will insist that whatever we claim to have discovered concerning the inherent distinction of something that we maintain lies beyond its mere appearance, is nothing more than the consequence of a vivid imagination induced by a neurological idiosyncrasy. This position the inevitable conclusion of an exclusively materialistic perspective. Unless a person of themselves has directly experienced their own inherent distinction and established it as their primary cognitive viewpoint, the material appears to be all there is. They must assume that the human, essential ipseity is a corporeally established designation and consequently they will not be able to recognize the intrinsic significance of things because their perspective will remain physically preoccupied.

The materialist will suppose that immediate engagement is no different from conventional objectivity although through the customary, cognitive approach we are unable to discern elemental existence or verify its authenticity. The only person able to know the significance of a direct ingress between the human, essential ipseity and the intrinsic nature of a phenomenon, is the one who has discovered it for themselves. All other opinion concerning the matter is basically moot because inevitably it will be established upon conjecture rather than empirically derived information. At best it may be founded upon impartial intelligence but without original experience the pertinence of immediate cognition will remain elusive.

The significance of the human, essential ipseity cannot be proven in the same manner as the substantiality of tangible phenomena but it can be demonstrated as extant through implication. This is the noblest assignment of art. A work of fine art will reveal the essential condition of a person or a thing while the material and corporeal circumstances remains underemphasized. The fine artist strives to articulate intangible relevancy through a particular medium of expression. Similarly, everything that is discerned concerning the intrinsic nature of existence through immediate cognition is found to be poignant because elemental circumstances are entirely meaningful and applicable. They are without superficiality because nothing that is essential is trivial.

The acceptance of the possible existence of the human, essential ipseity and the desire to explore the prospect of immediate cognition from the viewpoint of our own unique singularity, is antagonized in modern times because the discoveries resulting from the direct approach inevitably contradict exclusive, physically derived intelligence. That is to say, the suggestion of immanent volume is incomprehensible from a conventional, intellectual point of view because it is not merely antithetical but an entirely contradictory concept to the entrenched conviction of materialistic exclusivity.

The mentality that insists upon the physical predominance of existence, is established upon an abstract contrivance that is empirically, easily refuted. Yet materialism still retains its philosophical appeal because tangible circumstances are obvious and reciprocally confirmable. However, a merely physical depiction of life is void of meaning and pertinence through the shallowness of its perspective, and experience reveals the obvious, philosophical inadequacy of exclusive physicism.

When the physically elusive volume of things wherein poignancy and meaningfulness reside, is intellectually disassociated from phenomena we perceive life to be essentially monotonous, involuntary and void of implication. Obviously something vital is lacking from an exclusively materialistic depiction of existence because we readily experience intangible value in our ordinary lives. Therefore, a contradiction exists between materialistic philosophy and a familiar, human acquaintance with life itself which, conversely, we find to be full of intangible significances. The elusive proportion of phenomena requires an approach from an entirely different, essential perspective that is categorically negated by the conviction of material exceptionality.

For example, it is supposed that the quality of something is subservient to its physical condition and unrelated to its identification. The materialistic, scientific approach insists that two identical looking fruits, chemically analyzed and found to be equivalent, are indeed the same. Even if one is grown organically and is wholesome to eat while the other is chemically farmed and insipid, nevertheless, there is assumed to be no difference between the identities of the one over the other. But while they both appear to be alike through physical analysis, qualitatively the two are distinctly different fruits.

When we engage the essential nature of phenomena or of human beings, the authentic distinction is found to exist elementally, not physically. The elusive, intangible distinction between one thing and another is the authentic designation. Just as identical twins are found to be individually assertive and distinct in character in spite of appearances to the contrary, likewise, the essential significance of all things is intrinsic and physically obscure. Through immediate cognition, the human, essential ipseity recognizes the physically elusive condition that supersedes the material appearance. From the essential perspective, the obvious appearance of something does not reveal the fundamental identification.

11. Materialistic Myopia

Omnipresent *differs from **Ubiquitous** in meaning not merely everywhere, but present everywhere at the same time...**Universal** is a more general word which may be limited to correspond to everywhere; it means everywhere throughout the whole scheme of things.*

The viewpoint established when the human, essential ipseity is positioned as our principal identification, ensures the discovery of the elemental condition of things and the recognition of the intrinsic identification of ourselves and others. Essential existence resides not in the physical circumstances of phenomena, but it is immanently positioned in the same manner as our own intangible designation. We discover that the quiddity or quintessential significance of things exists within an intangible volume that is underestimated through a materially exclusive explication of existence because it is physically elusive.

Nevertheless, the physically elusive merit and intrinsic significance of something are its authentic expression of existence and inherent identification. The immanently, intangible volume of phenomena contains all that is meaningful and consequential. However, from the abstract perspective of materialistic, Western philosophy, physically imperceptible amplitude is a contradictory absurdity but in reality it is materialism that is contrived because it ignores the consequence of subtle significances. Bereft of the intrinsic dimension and innate constitution wherein the fullness of things resides, we find ourselves resigned to a merely superficial countenance that from an essential perspective, is an absurdly trivial designation.

Furthermore, in spite of the popular predilection towards abstract conjecture, materialistic philosophy does not withstand the practical challenge imposed upon it through the dynamic of human interrelationships wherein we quickly dismiss superficial exchanges as inconsequential. Yet, we fail to recognize the obvious disparity when a similar shallowness is implied towards existence as a whole but we continue to analyze the physical properties and blatant features of phenomena assuming that we will thereby determine their significance.

The depiction of an exclusively material state of existence void of an intangible dimension, is both an incomplete assessment established upon partial information and a deceptive device that has enormously disconsolate ramifications for humanity and for the subsequent preservation of the Earth that we inhabit. Regardless of human conviction to the contrary, reality itself is wisely constituted. It is only our interpretation of existence that is inclined towards the merely superficial semblance of things.

Through immediate, experiential engagement, we discover the human, essential ipseity and discern its incorporeal and enduring constitution. Furthermore, we recognize the condition of immanence wherein the essential significance of all things resides and we find that neither cessation, duration or physical magnitude have authority over it because emphatic existence is incommensurate with time and space. Thus, we recognize the essential, human condition as a continuum and that the constancy of the present is the authentic circumstance of intrinsic existence.

The direct recognition of essential continuity has far-reaching ramifications because the deception that the entirety of human existence is circumscribed within a restricted lifetime, is superseded. We find that mortal existence is not a capital conviction but a temporary expedient and we determine ourselves to be always appropriately positioned according to our mentality and demeanor. As soon as we redress our self-circumscribed deportment through openhearted reception to immanent caritas, inevitably our circumstances similarly accommodate the new disposition.

The significance of a direct recognition of essential continuity is that we find ourselves placed within circumstances that are optimum for our status and propitious to our advancement and eventual maturation.

Openhearted sincerity towards supernal caritas is not a mystical event but a practical expedient. It requires the establishment of a disposition of vulnerability not as an exercise or monotonous discipline but as a pragmatic alternative to the obsolete mentality of self-circumscription. It is astonishing that humanity remains protective of a segregated, petty sense-of-self when once the existence of immanent caritas and the possibility of the transformation of the human psyche, is intimated.

But the straightforward nature of things is frequently obscured through the assumption of an apparent foreknowledge and supposed acumen, when direct engagement alone is the appropriate recourse. The plain approach is concealed through misrepresentation because we assume that we can ascertain the nature of reality through deliberation and subsequent conviction. Sincere, openhearted vulnerability is the fitting resolution by virtue of its innocence and nothing short of simplicity and candor is suitable because if we are insincere, hollow or opinionated, obviously we cannot expect thereby to achieve impartially derived, authentic knowledge.

Similarly, the dynamic of a human transformation from a self-preoccupied myopia is obscured by considerable vagary on the part of supposed, religious authority. The remediation and subsequent advancement from self-circumscription towards modesty and unpretentiousness requires a sincere and receptive heart towards immanent caritas because it is within the soul that the discrepancy resides. However, the petty sense-of-self through its status of isolation, desperately masquerades as if it possessed some exceptional significance that must be doggedly safeguarded. But this inflated sense of consequence contradicts the discovery of the intrinsic self that is not anxious for importance because it experiences its emphatic continuance and finds that the same essential relevance is clearly the intrinsic distinction of everyone else.

12. The Petty Sense-of-Self

***Reasonable** is sometimes applied to persons in the general sense of having the faculty of reason. But more frequently the word **Rational** is used in this abstract sense of reason. In application to things reasonable and rational both signify according to reason; but the former is used in reference to the business of life, as a reasonable proposal, wish, etc.; rational to abstract matters, as rational motives, grounds, questions, etc.*

We do not possess the necessary capacity or aptitude to transform from a self-circumscribed disposition of estrangement and essential anxiety because we cannot conceive of a converse mentality except through our imagination.

Imagining something does not make it authentic and the abstract consideration of circumstances through the oblique approach of invention is a vastly remote cognitive practice from immediate experience. Indirect assessment, however rational and convincing cannot substitute for knowledge established upon direct, experiential engagement but it merely elaborates an already restricted perspective with further embellishment. Thus, inevitably, we further alienate ourselves from our essential distinction through an inveterate conviction that the petty sense-of-self is our legitimate singularity because experientially, that is all we know of our individuality.

We cannot banish the counterfeit sense-of-self through our own merit because it is a fundamentally and congenitally native conviction and we are compulsively defensive of its preservation. We recognize no other probable distinction beyond our banal mortality, and we lack the means to fashion one. But our impasse is founded upon an essential misperception that is unsupported in reality.

Through a restricted preoccupation with the tangible properties and the materially blatant proportion of things, we endeavor to construct an explanation of existence from a constricted and imperfect understanding. In operation, we find this representation thoroughly wanting but committed to the materially exclusive, scientific approach, we reasonably conclude that the dismal outcome of our research reveals the actual circumstances of existence. We fail to grasp that if our perception is entirely, materially derived, inevitably our conclusions will be similarly composed and tainted.

The concept of a perpetually progressive path of human development, epitomized in our time by extravagant technological innovation, is a fabrication without merit because it emphasizes an exclusively materialistic evolution. The advancement of humanity does not reside in the construction and production of equipment and merchandize but essentially, to the degree that we qualitatively transform towards our authentic identification.

Whenever we immediately and experientially engage the essential condition of a person or of a thing and discover its elemental significance, we enter into the immanent volume of existence. The immanent volume is where the intangible consequence of people and of phenomena resides, but it is obscured through an exclusive philosophy that only concedes to the merit of physical circumstances.

When we engage a phenomenon straightforwardly and immediately without assumed foreknowledge, we discover the essential distinction that epitomizes its existence. Through direct engagement we find the elusive, significance that is the elemental identification. Thus, the superficial appearance, cursorily perceived to be the consummate interpretation of something, is replaced by wisdom concerning the intrinsic condition.

An experience of the essential significance of a single phenomenon makes the entirety of intrinsic existence accessible because we only recognize the emphatic condition of things when we view them straightforwardly and immediately. Thus, we alter our perspective towards the detail and thereby establish the necessary terms required to engage all things essentially.

Within the condition of immediacy, we unaffectedly recognize the presence of an astonishing virtue that is diametrically and qualitatively opposed to our conventional, moribund mentality. It is distinctly evident that we ordinarily reside only within a segregated landscape, restricted within a narrow materialistically confined perspective with its concomitant, dismal repercussions upon our mentality and comprehension.

There is only one reality. The immediate, experiential engagement of the essential value of things puts our former standpoint under harsh scrutiny and we readily acknowledge the poverty of an existence composed of the merely perfunctory portion of things. Furthermore, the recognition of the authentic nature of existence changes the mundane appearance of things because we recognize their meaningful volume and more significantly, the unreality of our misperception.

The human, authentic constitution is maintained as an essential reality within the immanent dimension of existence because it is our actual status. But the petty sense-of-self hinders its recognition through self preoccupation and thereby detracts us from our natural development and necessary advancement.

All significance exists immediately and pettiness is only exceeded to the degree that we permit immanent caritas to emphasize the reality of our condition within the depths of a sincere and open heart. Thereby our concomitant insecurities that make us susceptible to all manner of aberration are dispatched and replaced here and now by the certainty of our authentic, constant existence within a boundless, magnificent universe. There are no other place and no other time. We are present as a continuum and it is from this viewpoint that we discover the authentic identification of one another and of all things.

13. Definitive Knowledge

*To **Know** is a general term; to be **Acquainted with** is particular. We may know things or persons in various ways; we may know them by name only, or we may know their internal properties or characters...Knowledge is a general term which simply implies the things known...The attainment of knowledge is of itself a pleasure independent of the many extrinsic advantages which it brings to every individual.*

Knowledge that is attained through immediate cognition is definitive because it pertains to the essential condition and authentic identification of things. Conventional perception offers only cursory apprehension, augmented by rationale and affective evaluation. We imagine that reason established upon astuteness and acumen, potentially supplies us with essential understanding because we assume that the physical appearance of things comprises their entirety. We do not realize that unless we engage circumstances immediately from the viewpoint of the human ipseity, we cannot discern the full extent of their existence.

The material condition is the incomplete, restricted proportion of a phenomenon, viewed without the physically elusive, essential volume. The transient state of something is without poignancy and pertinence because meaningfulness resides with the intangible portion that is imperceptible to an exclusively physical view.

For example, an invention remains intangible until it is physically expressed through manufacture. Without a concept there would be nothing to produce. We observe the product but we do not claim that it arose capriciously and independently of thought even though its origin is unrepresented in the appearance. Preoccupied with the palpable form, we overlook the conceptual origin because it is not readily apparent. But without physically inconspicuous creativity, there would be no physical appearance to observe.

The fundamental condition of a phenomenon is its intrinsic, elemental distinction. The reason why the human, essential ipseity is able to recognize elemental conditions is that it similarly exists in a physically elusive and original state. The human ipseity is not the consequence but resides at the source of material conditions in the same intrinsic realm as a concept or the elemental particularity of a native-element-mineral or of a color.

The essential ipseity establishes itself as the human, sovereign identification when assumed foreknowledge and the conventional, perceptive faculties of evaluation and rationale are restrained. Thereby, the intrinsic, individual human distinction recognizes itself and becomes positioned as the sovereign singularity of our constitution whose cognitive perspective is fundamental and absolute by virtue of its own elemental status. Thus, we come to recognize the authenticity of our own unique, essential distinction and that of others because we engage circumstances as they are, untarnished by predetermination or intellectual and affective deliberation.

The direct, cognitive approach is neither mysterious nor mystical but rests upon the realization of our authentic constitution. The elemental nature of the human, essential distinction is a fact of our existence. The recognition of singular ipseity inaugurates cognitive autonomy and subsequent liberation because we distinguish and identify the essential condition of things from the superficial.

Conventionally, we merely perceive a fraction of the full volume of existence because we are preoccupied with a materially circumscribed semblance that belies the essential nature of things. This is compounded by the conviction of an exclusively physical, human identification because our emancipation is obstructed if we assume that our identity is entirely physically confined. Thereby, we deny the human, essential ipseity that is the intrinsic nature of our constitution and, consequently, we abandon the possibility of our own cognitive and existential liberation. Furthermore, a perfunctory, materially preoccupied view degrades our mentality and subsequently we experience existence according to our innate, habitual demeanor and disposition towards life.

But it is not by our own efforts that we are delivered from this impasse. If it were, it would be the prerogative of only the very few while the majority of humanity would descend further towards an animalian, manic condition. However, a mandate is established upon our behalf, the inception of which requires merely our willing compliance. We position ourselves in the presence of supernal caritas through openhearted sincerity and embrace the institution of a new dispositional paradigm and perspective within the soul.

14. Acumen and Scholarship

*A **Consequence** is that which follows of itself, without any qualification or restriction; an **Effect** is that which is effected or produced, or which follows from the connection between the thing effecting, as a cause, and the thing effected. In the nature of things causes will have effects, and for every effect there will be a cause, although it may not be visible.*

Dependence upon our conventional cognitive faculties in order to research the state and conditions of essential reality, inevitably leads to uncertainty because rationale and affective evaluation function obliquely, but intrinsic existence is only directly apprehended through immediate engagement. Consequently, the contention between the precedent of physically substantiated fact over wishful thinking is moot from an essential perspective because knowledge through immediate cognition is not circumstantial but definitively ascertained. From the definitive viewpoint of the human, essential distinction, neither conviction nor calculation are the appropriate approach towards the discovery of intrinsic circumstances.

Unfortunately, we do not recognize that commensurate with the discovery and direct experience of the human, essential ipseity lies the capacity to discern and identify the nature of fundamental, physically elusive existence. It is assumed that our familiar, cognitive approach is the full extent of our ability. Therefore, we hone our logical processes and accumulate extensive acumen and scholarship assuming thereby that we are better equipped to identify the nature of existence. From a purely material point-of-view, this approach may be adequate, but the reliance upon exclusive physically derived information is misleading by virtue of the partial and abbreviated nature of the source.

Unavoidably, expertise exhaustively gleaned from the exclusive evidence of material conditions establishes a hierarchical order of authority. Accepted scientific and philosophical authority monopolizes the knowledge in a similar manner as those of religious scholarship and acumen, while the majority of people remain effectively ignorant and must trust the decrees of the elite.

The immediate engagement of circumstances puts our familiar, oblique cognitive approach into a very stark perspective and we recognize the inadequacy and banality of a methodology that is ostensively discerning but remains preoccupied solely with the analysis of conspicuous circumstances. Moreover, the practice of the associative correspondence of ideas embellished by abstract calculation, inevitably distances the thinker from the actual event and our thoughts become subsequently estranged from reality.

Customarily, human cognition depends upon an accumulated depository of prior appraisal augmented by rationale that is corrupted by individual preference established upon sentiment and predilection. We are only remotely concerned with the intrinsic distinction of things because the physical condition appears to be the most practical to us. We may painstakingly reduce, analyze and extract evidence concerning a situation but thereby we neglect the essential distinction of the entirety. We fail to engage circumstances originally and directly but, alternatively, we deliberate and ponder, collating and comparing our findings to predetermined data. Ignorant of the existence of the human, essential ipseity and the capacity of our intrinsic distinction to discern the elemental significance of things, we rely upon a conventional and restricted methodology that appears to be our highest cognitive capability.

Inevitably, through inadvertence and unfamiliarity with the intangible, meaningful volume as the overlooked significance of existence, we become preoccupied with our own perception and evaluation and thereby we fail to recognize the independent, inherent distinction of phenomena. Through preoccupation with the conspicuous semblance of things, a superficially constructed understanding is unavoidable because the value of phenomena does not reside in the physical appearance. The assumption that inceptive knowledge is to be found exclusively within the tangible structure, denies the significance of the origin.

Similarly, the assumption that we already know the nature of existence through our own evaluation and the analytical scrutiny of the obvious appearance of things, inhibits original engagement. It establishes a human interpretation of things where rightly we need to allow circumstances to remain pristine in order to attain impartial investigation. Immediate cognition requires an open, receptive posture that is uninfluenced by the presumption of the observer. Otherwise, we approach things preoccupied with a substitution of the real nature of things that does not serve us because it originates with ourselves and not the phenomenon.

That which we suppose and imagine that we know

from the material condition of things, even combined with accrued, associative erudition, is severely misleading because it impedes immediate and original engagement. Thus, our comprehension of existence is unsound and inevitably our philosophy and subsequent conduct will attest to its shallowness if we merely depend on the physical condition of things in order to ascertain their significance.

15. Value and Consequence

*When the question is to estimate the real qualities of persons or things, we exercise **Discernment**; when it is required to lay open that which art or cunning has concealed, we must exercise **Penetration**; when the question is to determine the proportions and degrees of qualities in persons or things, we must use **Discrimination**; when called upon to take any step or act any part, we must employ **Judgment**.*

The human, essential ipseity, through immediate engagement is able to discern the elemental significance of things including the intrinsic distinction of other people. Familiarity with the essential integrality of phenomena establishes before us an unequivocal exemplar of the profound constitution and meaningful proportion of existence. Thereby we are able to discriminate successfully between reality and remote, philosophical speculation.

We find the materialistic viewpoint that only appraises the tangible and corporeal conditions of things, to be superficial because it disregards the physically elusive extent of phenomena wherein significance and meaning reside. Materialistic, Western philosophy, in its architecture, dismisses all information that fails to correspond with tangible circumstances. However, the criterion that requires that something be physical in order to be considered relevant and included as pertinent to the evaluation of existence, contradicts common experience. Therefore the conclusions of an exclusive, physically established philosophy appear contrived and artificial against empirically derived knowledge. But through direct cognition, we penetrate beyond blatant evidence and discern the full significance of things. Subsequently, we establish a gauge or standard from which perspective we are able to decisively identify the value and merit of any ideological perspective. Direct experience of the relevancy and pertinence of the intangible dimension of material conditions precipitates a sensibility for legitimacy.

Conventional research and exploration involve the systematic and methodical scrutiny solely of the carapace of phenomena. Detached from the entirety, material circumstances are without meaning because abstracted from the physically imperceptible amplitude they merely represent a suspicion of the authentic condition. Thereby, the essential relevance of things is marginalized to the degree that it fails to correspond with tangible coordinates and subsequently, we find that our philosophical stance is bereft of humanly meaningful consequence and value.

Elemental distinction, that is the essential and authentic identification of things, is indiscernible from an exclusively physical outlook because it exists intangibly as the causal impetus of the material condition. Similarly, the conceptual origin and principles of organic organization can be recognized by their effects although they remain materially unidentifiable. Philosophy that is established upon the outward condition of things and which denies intrinsic motivation, is inevitably skewed respecting the mechanical characteristics because the approach emphasizes the visible workings and the physical properties. Consequently, existence is identified in terms of function, and our rendition of it inevitably depicts a soulless automaton.

The physically exclusive prejudice of materialistic, Western philosophy is profoundly unfavorable for the progress of humanity because it falsely establishes an abstractly conceived, moribund concept of existence in the place of reality. The substitution of a rawboned, philosophical abasement that has all meaning and value expunged from existence through materialistic restriction, renders the human condition lamentable because from an exclusively materialistic viewpoint life is justifiably recognized as pointless.

Immediate cognition reveals the essential substance of things, and their intrinsic pertinence becomes readily discernible. Thereby, through qualitative comparison, we find we are readily able to discriminate between materially established supposition and assumption, and the authentic condition of things. We recognize the irrelevancy of abstract, philosophical conjecture and religious doctrine because we directly experience the full context of the existence of phenomena.

Humanity is excessively preoccupied with the peripheral properties and material conditions of things to such a degree that we have come to assume that the body and the corporeal circumstances represent the entirety of the human constitution. But the authentic distinction is not solely mortal flesh and bone but an emphatic statement of perpetual existence. Furthermore, the essential ipseity is without biology and concomitant gender but finds itself only temporarily within an organic context because that is the fitting and compassionate status coincident with our prevailing mentality.

Immediate cognition from the viewpoint of the human essential ipseity enables us to directly engage circumstances without the distortion of conditioned perception. We recognize the unique distinction of ourselves and one another and thereby discern the physically elusive, elemental condition of all other things. However, the denial of the existence and significance of the essential identification of the human being prevents maturation and subsequent emancipation. The appalling deception of abstractly conceived constructs that purport to explain existence in physical terms, remain credible until the individual discovers the relevance of unique singularity and establishes essential ipseity as the human, sovereign distinction.

16. The Temper of the Soul

Chance *neither forms, orders nor designs; neither knowledge nor intention is attributed to it; its events are uncertain and variable...a person goes as chance directs...but chance cannot be calculated upon.* **Order** *lies in consulting the time, the place, and the object so as to make them accord; the* **Method** *consists in the right choice of means to an end...the* **Rule** *is that which is permanent and serves as a guide under all circumstances. A painter adopts a certain method of preparing the colors according to the rules laid down by his art.*

The recognition of human existence as a continuum whereby the essential identity of the individual perpetuates emphatically, consistently and constantly while corporeal and contextual conditions change, resembles in principle the characteristic, biological metamorphic cycle. For example, a butterfly remains intrinsically the same in nature whether it appears physical as an egg, a caterpillar or a chrysalis. However the clichéd metaphor of a transformation from grub to butterfly that suggest a paradisal afterlife misses entirely the significance of the comparison because it overlooks the necessity of an imperative amelioration of the human mentality.

Ordinarily, through the misrepresentation of materialistic, Western philosophy, we identify with the physical body and thereby assume that our unique distinction is merely, corporeally established. Thus, the hypothesis of a haphazardly instigated and arbitrarily selected, biological mutation that evolves into complex and fully functioning order, seems to make sense to us and we picture ourselves as the hapless victim or beneficiary of random events.

Immediate experience of the human, essential ipseity and the realization of its continuity, positions the human being crucially and autonomously within the dynamic of the transformation rather than as a victim of capricious circumstances. Through immediate cognition, as contrasted with abstract conjecture, we discover not chance, biological modification but the significance of our own stance and demeanor towards circumstances.

In Nature, it is the response of an organism towards ecological challenge and opportunity that provokes form change. These alterations necessarily occur within the parameters of accumulated, hereditary traits and characteristics. But the origin of the particular response and manner of accommodation is not incidental. It is determined by the idiosyncratic disposition of the creature towards circumstances. By this means, an animal cumulatively becomes an appropriate extension of a particular ecology and subsequently, it is inevitably and increasingly circumscribed within it.

The philosophical deception of human descent from primal simplicity through random selection, effectively denies and obscures human independence because it conceals the significant influence of our manner and dispositional inclinations upon the state of our soul. Subsequently, the qualitative condition of the human psyche etches a corresponding analogy upon the corporeal constitution, that is thereafter congenital. If that dynamic process of modification remains obscure and unrecognized by us then, inevitably, we assume ourselves to be prey to circumstances and not the author of our own destiny.

To the degree that we recognize how our manner and conduct influence the complexion of our psyche and correspondingly, alters our physical countenance and form within the ambience of our inherited proclivities and correlated appearance, we recover our autonomy. We discover that we participate in the quality and direction of our development. We recognize the crucial necessity of establishing a respectable, ethical posture and disposition in order that we may progress towards a more noble condition of heart. Those corrupt propensities that drag us downward towards the status of the instinctual animal while appropriate in zoology, are aberrations of the psyche for the human being. If indulged, they further ravage the soul and thereby precipitate human decline and bondage.

Thus, we recognize the compound nature of the deception that portrays the human being is merely another creature that mutated to sophistication from a simian ancestor. If we believe this farfetched and extravagant construction, then there is no possibility of progress and deliverance. Our maturation is entirely out of our hands and remains at the whim and caprice of impersonal forces.

In reality, the delusion of animalian status portrays the reversal of the actual circumstances. The human being has not arisen from the creature but is descending towards the beast through an abhorrent mindset that degrades and impoverishes the soul. The contrived philosophy of animalian origin has engendered self-indulgence in the name of personal liberation and an unhealthy sufferance towards cultural deterioration and depravity. The temper of the soul influences the human, existential stasis because our demeanor positions us appropriately within the befitting milieu. If we abandon restraint and rampantly pursue avaricious gratification, we establish ourselves within the same stratum as the creature. Furthermore, with the advantage of imagination, the human being can descend below animal innocence towards insatiable hedonism and the cruel maltreatment of others in the pursuit of a personal gratuity.

However, inherent within the fabric of existence resides the corrective for these deplorable circumstances. The remedy lies in the direct, cognitive experience of the constitution of things whereby we discover the legitimate nature of existence. Subsequently, we find that our singular identification resides not corporeally but essentially. Upon the discovery our authentic status we also recognize the unique ipseity of others and the elemental distinction of phenomena. Once having directly experienced the profound condition of existence, the counterfeit becomes odious to us and we yearn to elevate and reestablish our character in keeping with the quality of our essential nature. Accordingly, because these things are authentic, whereas formerly through ignorance we indulged an illusion, all the resources of existence inevitably work in accordance to elevate the human disposition to where it essentially resides. Merely through a willingness of heart, the human psyche is reestablished not through any merit of our own except for the longing to align ourselves with the way things really are.

17. Transilience

*We **Change** a thing by putting another in its place; we **Alter** a thing by making it different from what it was before; we **Vary** it by altering it in different manners and at different times. A thing is changed without altering its kind; it is altered without destroying its identity; it is varied without destroying the similarity.*

    We cannot independently craft an alternative disposition from congenital self-circumscription, without composite foreknowledge of the nature of the new condition. A conviction of exclusive isolation and separateness as the essential contingency of human existence is not dislodged without a profound reversal of perspective. From the status of self-interest, we are unable to conceive of an alternative, dispositional paradigm because the mentality of self-preoccupation is itself counter to our remediation.

    Conjointly with a moribund, subjective constitution that is established upon consternation concerning the survival of the petty sense-of-self, rests the misgiving that self-importance is merely an unsubstantiated pretense. Apart from the insistence of personal merit, there is little evidence and nothing in our power to corroborate personal value regardless of the commotion that we make to the contrary.

    Immediate engagement enables the human, essential singularity to discover the elemental conditions of phenomena that are otherwise overlooked from an exclusively materialistic perspective. Similarly, the innate individuality of each of us is able to distinguish the unique distinction of all other people through direct cognition. Thus, segregation and self-preoccupation are banished because we are mindful of the mutual significance of the human, essential distinction. Through this intelligence, we recognize the need for a profound reconstitution of both perspective and mentality.

The change that must occur in order that we may mature towards sovereign autonomy without counterproductively attempting to ignore a moribund disposition that is antithetical to liberty, is a reorientation of perspective away from a central subjectivity towards self-disinterest. Thereby, we become able to engage circumstances immediately and discover their intrinsic condition because we remove self-concern from our consideration.

Paradoxically, from the perspective self-abnegation we not only discover the essential condition of things but also identify our own authentic distinction. We find that the petty sense-of-self, that is circumspectly anxious and alert to its own maintenance, subsists upon an essential assumption that if it were neglected, it would become increasingly less significant and eventually destitute.

Self-preservation is entirely justified in terms of our physical status but from the moment that we discover and directly experience our essential distinction, we find that the vast, essential constituent of the human being lies impregnable within the immanent, intangible volume of existence. Therein, similarly reside the meaning and essential condition of all things that are otherwise elusive from an exclusively physical perspective. But through their permanency, essential circumstances are vastly more significant than the mere temporal.

It is the disparity between corporeality and physically indiscernible conditions that requires our attention because the relevance of things lies not in the appearance but with the emphatic, essential ambience. Inevitably, if we are preoccupied solely with the superficial countenance of something, the consequential portion will elude us. If we wish to engage elemental circumstances as they exist without the taint of human misconception, it is imperative that we acknowledge that conventional cognition is inadequate through the obliqueness of its approach.

Thus, we recognize the twin circumstances of the human condition that do not necessarily have to contradict. It is obviously foolish to neglect physical circumstances because we reside within a corporeal and material context. Conversely, if we aspire to a more profound relationship with existence we will become dissatisfied with the temporal because it is without the essential nourishment important to sustain our principal identification. The exclusively physical nature of things is transient but the material condition from the perspective of the human, essential status, is found to conceal an elemental distinction that is similarly immutable and appeals to our essential nature.

In terms of human emancipation from the myopia of materialistic, Western philosophy, the connection between the two perspectives will be recognized as one between appearances and essential significance. Through immediate cognition, we permit phenomena and circumstances to remain uninfluenced by our habitual, interpretative bias in order that we may recognize their intrinsic, elemental distinction. Inevitably, the blatant appearance of things becomes less compelling.

The practice of immediate cognition whereby the physically elusive significance of things is discerned, may also be applied in the area of the human conduct. Through our recognition of the essential, elemental condition of things and the unique distinction of one another, we engage circumstances not merely engrossed with the transient and superficial, but we transpose appearances through a profounder perspective.

Similarly, we recognize that the essential, human ipseity is not sustained by fugitive experience but is exhilarated by the sublime. Thus, we afford less attention to the apparent condition of things and seek instead the deeply profound significance.

It is the meaningful volume of existence that immanent caritas reveals to us through our openhearted willingness. But we also possess the capacity to engage Divinity from the perspective of our own unique and impeccable distinction. Through the attentive innocence that arises when we recognize our dependency upon a pansophical perspective instead of a humanly contrived explanation of existence, we directly experience the distinction of beneficent caritas itself through the human soul. We are otherwise helpless to progress and, in order that we may advance towards a meaningful destiny, we must seek an essential synchronicity within a susceptible and sincere heart.

Humanity did not self-originate and did we fabricate the human body. While the condition and timber of the soul influences the body towards health or disease, we can hardly accept ultimate culpability for our mutual plight because at this exigency we are without the means and inevitably compromise our own best interests through an inadequate constitution.

However, in reality we are not ill-equipped but merely ignorant of our own innate cognitive and moral aptitude. The emancipation of the human being is less a rescue but more significantly an inspiration and a pivotal progression. Within the realization of the existence and significance of the human ipseity lies extrication from the declining dignity of humanity but more particularly, it fosters an essential progression towards autonomy.

Susceptivity towards the beneficent influence of immanent caritas within the amenable, human heart is the resolution that we must assume in order that we may advance beyond self-circumscription. The possibility of a qualitative soul-transformation is provided for us as a decisive transaction that transverses an otherwise insurmountable predicament. It is wonderful but otherwise neither mystical nor a mysterious anomaly. The amelioration of the soul is an inherent dynamic that facilitates a natural longing towards maturation.

18. Assumed Foreknowledge

*The **Idea** is the simple representation of an object; the thought is the reflection; and the **Imagination** is the combination of ideas; we have ideas of the sun, the moon, and all material objects; we have thoughts on moral subjects; we have imaginations drawn from the ideas already existing in the mind. Ideas are formed; they are the rude materials with which the thinking faculty exerts itself; thoughts arise in the mind by means of association and combination...The term ideas is used in all cases for the mental representation, abstractedly from the agent that represents them...the thought occurs and reoccurs; it comes and it goes; it is retained or rejected at the pleasure of the thinking being.*

Imagination needs to be recognized and applied in accordance with its innate capacity to conceive and invent otherwise unconventional circumstances. In terms of existential knowledge, it has no place whatsoever because imaginary is superseded by direct engagement and the subsequent identification of actual circumstances.

Imaginative representation is not reality. Reality is the condition of authenticity that may be grasped conceptually through a stretch of the imagination but it otherwise remains unknowable except through immediate cognition. There exists only reality while everything else is abstract imagery.

In order to discover the authentic distinction of something, we must engage circumstances without foresight or association. Thereby we are no longer preoccupied with symbolic ideas concerning events, but we experience the actual phenomena, immediately, as they exist inherently, of themselves.

Immediate cognition without the confusing influence of imaginative association repositions our identification away from self-circumscription and into the context of the essential condition of things. The essential is the reality as opposed to the superficial appearance or hypothetically conceived status of something.

Imagination is a function of the human, corporeal constitution while, conversely, reality having no necessity of inventive clarification or conceptual explanation, exists emphatically irrespectively of our ideas concerning it. Through our reliance upon understanding rather than direct experience by immediate, cognitive engagement, we are generally unaware of the capacity of the human ipseity to instantly discern essential conditions. Instead, we have established an impression of existential comprehension through oblique perception that contradicts reality.

The conceptual structures that we have assembled and devotedly follow even in the face of contradictory evidence, are established upon an assortment of chosen criteria. Even amongst a common affiliation, there is seldom consistency except in the most generally acceptable term because rationale is idiosyncratic. Accordingly, the deductive discipline of science has become the popular alternative and its overuse as a panacea for subjective rationale has become almost a cliché. It is thought that the practice wherein we discover the principles of physical law by systematic trial and error, is applicable to the interpretation of essential existence.

Consequently, a cognitive approach that is ideally and successfully appropriate to the exploration of the physically apparent conditions of things, establishes a physical, conceptual structure that is overtly materialistic in nature and leans heavily towards mechanisms and processes. The resultant interpretation of existence inevitably resembles an automated and impersonal contrivance. If evidence is produced, that is unsuitable to physical scrutiny, it is discarded as subjectively derived and therefore any challenge to materialism is easily deflected.

Materialistic bias has become ingrained through a popular enthusiasm with technological invention and innovative creativity. But, however systematic the approach, if a standardized examination of evidence is only applicable to the workings of things it remains insufficient when turned upon nonphysical circumstances. The resultant conclusions are inevitably misleading and predictably, the philosophical formulations that arise from an exclusively physical examination of circumstances, do not assist but hinder human progress through their narrow perspective.

The necessary dismissal of evidence that is intangible in nature and unsuitable to physical examination, reveals the shortcomings of the scientific approach in matters that pertain to essential existence because elemental immutability is only peripherally, physically represented. But the conceptual edifice that represents a physically exclusive universe remains intact because it is supported by peer consensus that is restrictive of any intelligence other than that which is materially founded. The materialistically established philosophy is virtually impregnable because it only accepts information upon its own materialistic terms. Thus, even an obviously unprovable hypothesis such as the descent of biological complexity from a rudimentary morphon, which is an untenable abstraction from the perspective of common sense and matter-of-fact reflection, is supported by the majority of the scientific community.

Therein we find an imaginative interpretation of existence that is permitted to supersede even innate intelligence because of the accumulated weight of circumstantial, material evidence. This lamentable situation has arisen merely through ignorance concerning the significance of the human, essential distinction and its residence within the immanent, meaningful volume of existence. If through a materialistically skewed scientific discipline that we conclude that human kind is solely, corporeally constituted and that the physical condition and circumstances of things comprise the entirety of their existence Thereby we hinder our further advancement. That is to say, through a constricted preoccupation with the obvious appearance of things we overlook the essential.

19. Beyond Physical Coordinates

***Directly** is most applicable to human action; **Immediately** and **Instantly** to either actions or events...Immediately and instantly, or instantaneously, both mark a quick succession of events, but the latter in a much stronger degree than the former...Immediately expresses simply that nothing intervenes; instantly signifies the very existing moment in which the thing happens...A course of proceeding is direct, the consequences are immediate, and the effects are instantaneous.*

From a perspective that is solely preoccupied with physical conditions and material appearances, it is impossible to recognize the essential distinction that is the authentic identification of phenomena because it is materially imperceptible. The location of intrinsic significances, for example, is a moot consideration because physical parameters are incommensurate with essential existence. Consequently, the familiar coordinates that circumscribe material conditions are insufficient when applied to intrinsic distinctions because fundamental significance is implicit but otherwise physically unrepresented.

The essential distinction of something is the authentic appellation that determines the inherent particularity that is not discernible in the conspicuous appearance but merely implied. Size, for example, is irrelevant in terms of the qualitative and characteristic condition of a thing. Consequently, intrinsic pertinence cannot be discovered and identified by conventional, physically circumscribed cognition but it is found only through the immediate engagement of the phenomenon. The conceptual origin of a humanly manufactured item serves as a fitting example of the significance of intangible continuance.

We are thoroughly accustomed to material conditions and establish our reasoning within those constraints. Accordingly, it is extraneous to describe a condition that is without physical correlation to those unwilling to explore beyond the palpable. A conceptual viewpoint will hinder the direct cognition of something and thereby we will continue to suppose phenomena to be other than they really are. To the inflexible materialist, everything real must be physically qualified in some fashion otherwise it is condemned as merely amorphous and indeterminate imagination.

Exclusive attention to the physical condition of things obscures the essential dimension because implicit distinction exists intangibly. The material status of something is readily obvious while, for example, the quality or the merit of something is more difficult to ascertain and to evaluate. Intangible value is not physically apparent and cannot be ascertained solely from the material appearance.

According to banal materialism, the reduction of phenomena into elementary constituents and the quantification of physical characters is thought to be a more reliable indicator of the particularity of something than subjective experience. Thus, a systemized, analytical approach that vigorously advocates the blatant, physical condition takes precedent, while the testimony of human, direct cognitive experience is frequently viewed with suspicion and cast into doubt.

An exhaustive scrutiny of the physically perceptible properties of things can never reveal anything other than information regarding the atrophied status because the structure is emphasized at the expense of elusive value. If we examine once more the example of a humanly conceived and manufactured item, it is immediately apparent that the product alone only indirectly represents the conceptual origin and the particular, qualitative significance of the materials of which it is comprised. But consideration of the elusive, imperceptible extension and conceptual origination of an item reveals the intangible, capacious dimension that is imperceptible if the merely physical properties of the commodity comprise the circumference of our inquiry.

We do not usually recognize the intrinsic significance of phenomena because we are distracted by the conspicuous appearance. An overconfident, materialistically partisan approach towards existence causes us to doubt our own direct experience because the authority of the technological community appears to overwhelm our own judgment. The stigma of appearing unreasonable and arbitrary in our deliberation in the face impressive, scientific perspicacity promotes a passive acquiescence and we dismiss our own experience as uninformed.

Our hesitation is justified unless we develop the ultimately objective approach of immediate cognition. Thereby we set aside all predisposition and assumed foreknowledge and engage circumstances straightforwardly in order that we may discover their intrinsic distinction and essential complexion. The object of our inquiry is encountered without the distortion of personal penchant and proclivity because we are determined to discover the intrinsic distinction that is the authentic designation.

The physical conditions of phenomena are readily perceptible and through detailed scrutiny we supposed that the essential significance is similarly evident within the minutiae. But the intrinsic pertinence of an object does not reside structurally or anatomically. It exists by implication but is otherwise not materially apparent. Predictably, the location where the essential meaning and connotation of existence is found is not dimensionally dependent but immediate because intrinsic significance resides not spatially but immanently.

20. Human, Essential Distinction

***Incorporeal** marks the quality of not belonging to the body or having any properties in common with it...The earth, sun, moon etc., are termed **Material**; but the impressions that they make on the mind, that is, our ideas of them, are immaterial...material is used for everything which can act upon the senses, animate or inanimate. The world contains corporeal beings, and consists of material substances.*

The quintessential distinction of things is physically elusive but otherwise of crucial implication. We may analyze and isolate the idiosyncratic properties of something, but we cannot find intrinsic significance in the material condition because while essential value has physical extension, it is not explicitly found within the material construction.

We do not usually recognize the intrinsic circumstances of phenomena because we are preoccupied with physical characteristics and naturally assume that the pertinence of things rests upon their material attributes. Thereby we entirely overlook the intangible dimension that possesses the distinctive particularity and elemental disposition. The essential nature of things is of greater consequence than the physical constitution because intrinsic distinction exists categorically and unambiguously. The unequivocal identity of something is found not within the dimension and amplitude or the material circumstances that describe it, but, conversely, it possesses an emphatic distinction wherein proportion is irrelevant.

The intrinsic significance and authentic identification of phenomena, while expressed through the appearance, are not found in the material circumstances themselves but within the manner and disposition of the physical expression. For this reason, the actual nature of things is physically unrepresented although it remains the impetus for the appearance and the particular properties. The conclusive appellation is found through immediate cognition because it exists immanently as the origin of the characteristic, physical circumstances, in the same manner as the human, essential ipseity.

Thus, we meet another human being either superficially, whereby we assume that the appearance and biology comprise their entire identification, or essentially and recognize their unique distinction. If our communication is established upon a merely cursory perception, our exchange will be similarly perfunctory and the other person will know it.

This will seem an obvious observation to anyone whose mentality is unclouded by an abstractly conceived and materially entrenched philosophy towards existence because we recognize the distinction between the trivial approach and the essential, through accumulated experience. But materialistic, Western philosophy denies the existence of the human, essential distinction because it is intangible and fails to be identified by the test of physical substantiation. Abstractly premeditated, the human essence is imagined to be synonymous with the biology and the evidence of direct experience to the contrary is dismissed.

Everything that is acceptable to the materialistic mentality must conform with the criterion of physical representation. Consequently, if something appears to possess an even indirectly quantifiable property that is amenable to mensuration, it is solely that constituent possessed of physical inference that is isolated and thought to comprise the entirety. It is scarcely any wonder that under such partiality we establish a contrived worldview that is entirely at odds with our own experientially established judgement.

The reason for the intensity of discrimination if favor of the superficial is that the physical condition of something it readily plausible and justifiable while the intangible essential is not physically ascertained. We are anxious concerning subjective experience because of the human propensity to commingle inventive imagination and wishful thinking and establish an unfounded belief system that is entirely conjectural.

But immediate cognition from the viewpoint of the human, essential ipseity, constrains the imagination similarly as it restricts abstractly conceived interpretations of existence. It is able to distinguish the essential significance of a phenomenon from the peripheral semblance because its own existence is similarly absolute. Thus, it directly engages the elemental and conclusive distinction of all other phenomena and entities.

Only cold, abstract Cartesian logic would seriously question the existence of material circumstances but intellectual, detached conjecture is recognized as similarly tenuous when it fabricates a contrived philosophy that contradicts common experience. Modern, standardized scientific-methodology relies upon the exclusive evidence of physical circumstances and thereby constructs an artificial account of existence that is superficially derived and consequently inadequate. A philosophy that overlooks the significance of the intangible, intrinsic distinction of things is inattentive. But through immediate cognition, the human, essential distinction discovers the missing amplitude and consequence of the existence of things and is impatient with the merely physical perspective because it finds no value in the superficial view.

21. The Original Encounter

__Instant__...to stand over, signifies the point of time that stands over us...__Moment__...momentum, to move, signifies properly movement, but is here taken for the small particle of time in which any movement is made. Instant is always taken for the time present; moment is taken generally for either past, present or future...When they are both taken for the present time, instant expresses a much shorter space than moment.

The instant, as a continuous point in time, describes the whereabouts of the overlooked, meaningful volume of material conditions. Therein lie the indispensable pertinence of existence and the elemental distinction of all things. The continuum of the moment is conceptually incommensurate with our understanding of material circumstances. However, although recognition of physically elusive conditions does not gainsay the existence of the material proportion of our surroundings, conversely, we are habituated towards and most readily accommodate our corporeal and physical ambiance at the expense of the intrinsic significance of things.

Without the recognition of the intrinsic value and distinction of things, existence appears capricious and we find order only in the function and predictable regularity of its workings. But there is no purpose or meaning solely in contrivances. We merely discover procedures and mechanical structures that are without direction or accountability beyond the inevitable, causal nexus of impersonal events.

It is upon this selective thinking that materialistic,

Western philosophy has arisen. Without the direct cognizance of the essential volume of existence that resides within the moment, we have contrived a rationale that is established exclusively upon physically qualifiable evidence. It is the only verifiable information that we have because of the inherent limitations of a congenital, materialistically exclusive myopia. Even religious conviction fails to successfully argue under those terms and must rely instead upon doctrinal confidence and personal faith.

Upon the basis of a particular scholarship, the academician supposes that through accumulated acumen within a certain area of expertise, an authority over the constitution of the nature of all existence necessarily follows. It is hard indeed, to imagine that a gardener or carpenter would assume a similar prerogative even after a lifetime of empirically derived wisdom and by the practical competence of their occupation. Yet, the reasonable and systematic mind of the layman may be as qualified as the professor to evaluate life through direct experience and realistic commonsense because intellectual sharpness is moot in terms of immediate experience.

But an academic collegiate, whose expertise resides within very narrow parameters, assumes a right of discrimination concerning matters even beyond their particular field of proficiency. That which grants the learned and scientifically accomplished command in one particular area is assumed to qualify them in matters otherwise unexplored except in very casual terms. But intellectual cleverness and cultivation sanctions deference and consequently the unschooled are expected to relinquish their independency to the expert in much the same way as ecclesiastical authority held sway over the illiterate of former centuries.

The deductive rationalism of the intellectual, augmented by accumulated scholarship, has become the acceptable and consistent approach of the philosophical materialist towards all circumstances. But the detached, analytical position is insufficient when applied to matters that cannot be argued through abstract deduction but are only experientially discernible. Intellectual comprehension and logical argumentation are incompatible to matters that must be directly encountered and experientially explored in order to be known.

An understanding of the significance of the moment as an access point to an elemental continuum that is physically imperceptible, is unproductive if the mastering of a concept is the extent of our inquiry. The abstract, scientific theorist constructs similarly abstruse propositions without confirmation or conclusive evidence. Accumulated intellectual sophistication is no measure of familiarity with essential existence but neither is cognizance without direct experience.

The manner whereby we may discover the essential circumstances respecting human existence and that of our Earthly context, is through pristine engagement. Unsophisticated observation, uncorrupted by the assumption of foreknowledge and partisan assessment, permits an original encounter whereby the human, essential distinction is able to unaffectedly approach circumstances in their elementary condition.

It is not possible to recognize the unembellished state of phenomena if we convey and transfer our own assessment and speculation regarding their character and purpose. We merely complicate and conceal the ingenuous approach with pretension and, subsequently maintain our own suspicions and speculations in preference to what is really there. Thereby we obscure the original encounter and fail to discover the legitimate, existential circumstances.

Paradoxically, the direct, experiential recognition of human, essential ipseity as positioned within the present continuum, reestablishes our attention and sensibility towards the potency of the moment. We find that immediacy, fertile with significance, instructs us concerning the physically elusive volume of existence because, through straightforward, unambiguous cognition, the elemental distinction of things is discovered.

22. The Transformative Event

__Transfigure__ is to make to pass over into another figure; __Transform__ and __Metamorphose__ are to put into another form...Transformation is commonly applied to that which changes its outward form; in this manner a harlequin transforms himself into all kinds of shapes and likenesses. Metamorphosis is applied to the form internal as well as external; that is, to the whole nature; in this manner Ovid describes, among others, the metamorphosis of Narcissus into a flower and Daphne into a laurel.

The qualitative comparison between circumstances viewed through immediate cognition as opposed to conventional perception, allows us to determine the discrepancy between knowledge derived through an examination of the material conditions of things, with essential circumstances. Thereby we readily recognize deception when we see it and establish a benchmark from our own direct experience, composed of that which constitutes significance.

A turbid distillation of existence, perceived within the limits of physical parameters, distorts our view of the authentic constitution of both ourselves and phenomena. But when we become familiar with the characteristic nature and condition of essential existence, we are no longer deceived by an inadequate outlook nor by compounded, abstract interpretations that further fictionalize the original misperception.

Immediate cognition replaces the conventional concept of time with observance of the continuous moment wherein circumstances are engaged and negotiated not obliquely but immanently. It is in the present moment that the poignancy and profound significance of a situation is revealed and directly experienced. We find that all events are entirely appropriately positioned for our instruction towards existential autonomy and liberation.

Every occurrence engaged directly in the moment, becomes a transformative event because circumstances are experienced from the perspective of intrinsic existence which is occupied by the human, essential ipseity and the beneficence of supernal caritas. Thus, we inevitably relinquish the moribund disposition of the petty sense-of-self that is established upon disquiet and foreboding, for magnanimity.

Even past events can be brought within the continuous moment whereby understanding and subsequent clemency replaces resentment. This is authentic forgiveness and it occurs without reservation.

The human, essential distinction never changes because it is our authentic identification. But our mentality and demeanor must and will transform within the immanent moment because our stance becomes realigned with the authentic circumstances of existence. When we discover things as they really are instead of how we perceive and imagine them to be, our former misapprehension is recognized as erroneously established.

Imagination removes our attention away from the immanent present. It is a faculty that if misused, replaces immediacy with a fictional substitute. If innovativeness and ingenuity are indulged and distort our view of actual circumstances, they work against our best interest because unreality does not exists except as a chimerical absurdity. Existence must be engaged as it really is and not as we visualize it to be. Sadly, the illusory view is the source of the deplorable plight and the compound ignorance of human kind. However, we find ourselves in the ideal circumstances where the delusion may become increasingly fractured because the specious view does not correspond with reality and it is consequently untenable in practice.

Upon every occasion that we fail to engage circumstances in the immanent present, we re-embrace the delusion and thereby we find ourselves subject to apprehensive isolation because falsity is necessarily estranged from reality. Upon the heels of the perception of individual, essential segregation, comes a concomitant distortion towards all other circumstances because our dominant premise towards existence inherently disagrees with reality.

It is within the instant that we directly engage supernal caritas through openhearted sincerity. Within the immanent present, all sustenance and support are directly available, and it is the achievement of the immediate condition of concurrence that is the highest expression of prayer and our assurance of the dispositional transformation of the soul. Thereby the human, obsolete mentality of self-circumscription is abandoned because it was unsubstantiated in reality anyway, notwithstanding a former conviction to the contrary.

23. Immediacy

***Visible** is used purely in a physical sense; apparent...is used physically...and morally(archaic usage meaning an ostensible or seeming characterization). That which is simply an object of sight is visible; that which presents itself to our view in any form, real or otherwise, is **Apparent**; the stars themselves are visible to us; but their size is apparent. Visible is applied to that which merely admits of being seen; apparent...denotes not only what is to be seen...but is an epithet to objects of mental discernment...A thing is apparent on the face of it.*

The conspicuous countenance of things is corrupted by the practice of approximating newly discovered situations and phenomena with familiar, comparable reminiscence. They are further obscured through the establishment of definition and exposition that describes and defines what something is and thereby replaces the actual circumstances with a conceptual substitute. Even a name serves as a pseudopodium for the thing itself.

The manner whereby we customarily describe what something is does not necessarily touch upon its intrinsic significance but usually pertains only to its material properties and functions. Thus, we associate phenomena perfunctorily upon the basis of their physical characteristics and assume that we have thereby successfully identified them. Inevitably, the essential distinction influences the appearance, but otherwise it resides intrinsically and it is not physically apparent.

The particular singularity of a phenomenon, that is

the authentic identification, is not obviously recognizable from a scrutiny of the material characteristics. It is far more subtle, and resides constitutionally as the especial nature and temper that instigates the particular appearance. It is the qualitative distinction whereby something inherently and particularly exists. It is the person or the object's *this-ness or formal distinction* as formulated by John Duns Scotus (1266 – 1308). If the *this-ness* were of any other quality, it would cease to possess the same identity.

The manner whereby we identify and describe the material condition of things is necessarily physically dependent. But the physically elusive, essential distinction is depicted through the metaphoric language of fine art.

A particular color or mineral possesses intrinsic distinction that determines its characteristic exposition. Regardless of the context where it is found, the color red, for example, always maintains the same expression. The essential distinction of something is its authentic identification as opposed to the material carapace. Thus, we recognize that the intrinsic significance of phenomena precedes the physical properties that comprise its appearance. The actual identity is possessed of elemental volume and emphatic existence that contradicts the material transience. The distinction between the appearances of something as opposed to the elemental significance is similar to that of an oblique reflection in contrast to an inceptive, categorical statement.

Lifeforms also possess an intrinsic distinction that determines the manner of their particular appearance.

The physical constitution is determined by an archetypal, structural precedent to which the organism must conform in order to remain viable. It is a universal, organic standard that is malleable not in principle but in application. But the idiosyncratic nature and particular timbre of expression belong to the distinction of the creature itself.

The unique distinction that is the authentic identity of the human being, is independent of the organism. The body is structured and functions according to the universal principles of the organic archetype. All organisms share in the same fundamental, biological infrastructure albeit differently disposed according to the particular application and ecology.

The human, essential ipseity resides not within physical parameters but occupies the immediate condition of the immanent present. Therein reside the intrinsic distinction of everything else including the unique identity of a color, a mineral and conceptual, biological origin. This is not another place but it is the intangible, overlooked volume that is the meaningful inception of the physical semblance. If we are preoccupied with mere appearances, our perception remains shallow and our comprehension, void of significance and essential relevance.

From the viewpoint of the immediate present, we discern the intrinsic distinction of all other things. But most significantly for humanity, we may also enter into an instructive and restitutive concurrence with immanent caritas that guides us towards the fulfillment of our destiny.

We find through sincere open heartedness, a

profound and expanding devotion towards immanent caritas because a tenderness arises within the soul that supplants our former isolation and uncertainty. We inevitably discover the presence of kindness through openhearted unanimity, and we become immeasurably assured and gratified.

One of the significant obstacles against establishing an essential intimacy with immanent caritas and making the human soul susceptible to reorientation, is ignorance of the existence and nature of immediate continuance. Habitually, we consider things from an exclusively material perspective including religious concepts concerning an ethereal realm, which presents us with an irresolvable contradiction. Consequently, we wonder where on Earth or in the heavens the so-called spiritual realm resides. In fairness, we must either abandon our trust in the existence of a celestial realm or conversely we must question the substance and consequence of material circumstances.

Immanence is not approachable through our conventional understanding. Furthermore, it cannot be demonstrated as extant through deduction and deliberation. It is an essential condition that must be straightforwardly experienced in order to be recognized and verified. It is not bound within the familiar coordinates of space nor influenced by duration but it exists emphatically, accessible only through the immediate engagement of the human, individual distinction.

24. Open-mindedness

***Benevolence** is literally well willing. **Beneficence** is literally well doing. The former consists of intention, the latter of action: the former is the cause, the latter the result. Benevolence may exist without beneficence, but beneficence always supposes benevolence...As benevolence is an affair of the heart, and beneficence of the outward conduct, the former is confined to no station, no rank, no degree of education or power: the poor may be benevolent as well as the rich, the unlearned as the learned, the weak as well as the strong; the latter on the contrary, is controlled by outwards circumstances, and is therefore principally confined to the rich, the powerful, the wise, and the learned.*

Immanently present caritas, dispels human isolation and subsequent disquiet. It dissipates self-circumscription and supersedes the priority of self-importance that has become established through the demands of biological perpetuation and respective survival.

We find that we no longer wish to be segregated, self-absorbed and preoccupied with the constricted perspective of the petty sense-of-self. Rationalization and speculation are subsequently displaced by knowledge concerning the essential significance of things and we come to deplore superficiality and perfunctoriness because we experience the meaningfulness of things. We wish to discover the way things really are.

Furthermore, upon our first glimpse of the significant volume of phenomena after a long and habitual acquaintance with only a very shallow perception of existence, we are struck by the almost overwhelming richness of essential pertinence. Everything is found to possess a more profound implication because we directly engage the intrinsic identification and particular value instead of merely the material circumstances. Thereby, all things are found to possess particular distinction.

The particular distinction of phenomena is entirely juxtaposed to information derived from conventional systematics because ordinarily we merely describe things upon the merit of their obvious, physical properties. We remain ignorant and removed respecting essential distinction because we are distracted by structure, contrivance and function. We imagine that a phenomenon is correctly identified upon the basis of what it does and the mechanics of that execution. Subsequently, we categorize things upon the basis of the physical assets of the appearance, and we fail to recognize the elemental distinction.

Essential significance is not established upon the physical details of something but inversely, the material conditions are the consequence of the unique designation that is alike to an inherent, elemental signature. In this sense, a phenomenon such as the color red or a native-element-mineral, possesses an essential distinction that more properly resembles an entity than a list of physical properties and concomitant activities and functions.

The essential distinction of something is a particular identity rather than a consolidation of properties. If the color red was merely the sum of its physical properties, it would be senseless to attribute specific distinctness to it because it would be without comprehensive cohesion. It would not possess identity established upon its entirety but according to fragmentary evidence. If we assume that something is only composed of an aggregate of particulars and minutiae such as molecules, atoms or quanta, then the suggestion of intrinsic identification would be absurd.

From the foregoing reasoning, it is evident that we must inevitably fail to recognize the intrinsic integrity of a phenomenon if our approach is predominantly analytical because we do not engage the entirety wherein the authentic distinction resides. But if we abandon the usual oblique, piecemeal approach and restrain partisan preference, we will inevitably find ourselves face to face with the essential distinction because we thereby view the phenomenon in its elemental integrity without the distortion of human interpretation.

Through immediate cognition, we depart from the usual inclination to identify phenomena through reduction, analysis and rationale because the conventional methodology obscures direct engagement. Further, it is of no interest to us to approach circumstances from a perspective of tendentious partiality because a partisan assessment will offer nothing of consequence but merely serve to further detract from candid and dispassionate investigation.

Our aim is straightforward open-mindedness and we have no interest whatsoever in wishful thinking or guesswork. These things are already apparent from the confused manner of conventional cognition. That is, it is entirely counterproductive to the direct discovery of elemental conditions, to second-guess the significance of our experiences because there is no merit in conjecture and postulation. We desire to straightforwardly discover the authentic constitution of existence and nothing less will suffice.

25. Oblique Thinking

__Definite__ signifies that which is defined, or has the limits drawn or marked out; __Positive__ that which is placed or fixed in a particular manner...in respect to others, the more definite the instructions which are given the less danger there is of a mistake; the more positive the information communicated the greater the reliance which is placed upon it.

Immediate cognition occurs in a scrupulous vacuum in the sense that all presupposition concerning a particular phenomenon under investigation, is set aside. Through the conventional cognitive approach whereby we associate new experiences with affiliated ideas and recollections, the concise distinction of something is overlooked. Furthermore, the establishment of hypotheses and theory to fill the gaps in order that, through observation and experimentation we might discover the fundamental mechanics, detracts from direct engagement.

The viewpoint of immediate cognition is through the essential ipseity that is the human, singular distinction. It is absolute and exists essentially. Consequently, it recognizes the elemental condition of everyone and everything else.

The conventional cognitive approach occurs circuitously and inevitably our conclusions are ambiguous and inconclusive because we have to appraise and estimate the significance of our findings. This is because we are not approaching the imperative distinction of things that possesses definite identity but we merely explore the peripheral properties through our accustomed methodology.

In this light we recognize the pervasiveness of compound hindrances that obscure the practice of immediate cognition. We are ignorant of essential significances and consequently we do not anticipate the existence of an intangible volume wherein meaningfulness resides. Furthermore, we are excessively preoccupied with material conditions and have become convinced that the physical is the full extent of reality. Thus, we approach existence obliquely endeavoring to estimate and interpret a situation upon the basis of its merely tangible assets.

If we do not distinguish our own inherent singularity then concomitant, immediate cognition is accordingly obscured through ignorance. Inevitably, we endeavor to interpret and evaluate the human condition using the limited means of the intellect, imagination and the affective preference because they are apparently the only devices at our disposal.

But the conventional approach is only adequate if we wish to explore the physical conditions of things and isolate their properties. Inevitably, we remain ignorant of the essential distinction because it precedes and anticipates the blatant appearance. We are unable to discover the meaningful significance of one another and of phenomena because they are unrecognizable from an exclusively material consideration.

Usually, we exhaustively glean, interpret and evaluate information hoping to amass extensive data upon which to establish our understanding. But assessment by virtue of its oblique approach, is always ambiguous regardless of the quantity of details that we are able to compile. Without a faultless benchmark of what constitutes reality, we must inevitably surrender to a deductive rationale that is antithetical to definitive identification.

Unless we apply calculation to the quantifiable, physical properties of things, there is no possibility of exactitude because deduction and rationale are not exact disciplines. But the mensuration and the calibration of blatant particulars is an incommensurate approach to the discovery of the essential distinction of phenomena because our results inevitably resemble those mathematically susceptible aspects from which our research is derived.

If we scrutinize phenomena from a purely physical perspective and attempt to ascertain their essential significance, we may identify how something functions and the ostensible purpose of a particular operation but we remain ignorant of what a thing essentially is. Neither a color nor a native-element-mineral has workings, accordingly the physicist searches within the molecular structure and there discovers electrical activity upon which the definition of the particular substance can be established. But subatomic motion is not synonymous with the intrinsic particularity of something anymore than the workings of the body represent the human, individual identification.

When we explore the nature of phenomena from the consideration of function, we inevitably establish a systematics upon mechanics and assume that the manner of operation is the authentic identity. Similarly, if we consider the material appearance and mensurable properties as our basis of classification, we merely appraise the superficial properties wherein there is no intrinsic meaning.

Whenever, we conduct ourselves towards other people from the hypothetical conviction that they are merely biological, we contradict our own experience to the contrary and deny human, essential significance. All bodies function alike and we cannot differentiate between one person or another except in terms of an aggregate of organic minutiae that does not possess essential identity.

Materialistic, Western philosophy is established upon the superficial appearance and the utility of things. It is a contrived, abstract assessment of existence devised obliquely from the immediate circumstances.

Through the exhaustive analysis of physical conditions, essential significance remains obscure because it must be approach directly and experientially. If we commence the exploration of phenomena, mentally prepossessed by the mere mechanical conditions and physical properties, we will never discover the intrinsic distinction of things upon which the meaningfulness of material circumstances depends. Our conclusions will be inevitably slanted according to the narrow manner of our approach. Thereby we obscure the possibility of finding essential significance because our attention is preoccupied and fascinated with the surface appearance.

26. Receptivity

***Sentiment** has its seat in the heart, the **Sensation** is confined to the senses, and **Perception** rests in the understanding. Sentiments are lively, sensations are grateful, perceptions are clear. Gratitude is a sentiment most pleasing to the human mind: the sensation produced by the action of electricity upon the frame is generally unpleasant; a nice perception of objects is one of the first requisites for perfection in any art.*

Immediate cognition requires that all presumption, theory and philosophical posture, be restrained and that we approach phenomena from a position of ignorance as to their essential significance. In other words. The intrinsic distinction of something is the authentic identification that exists elementally and immanently but it is imperceptible if we are immersed and preoccupied with our own particular account and understanding of things. We must assume a straightforward and unpretentious inquiry.

Our approach must be untainted and pristine otherwise we will be preoccupied with our own opinion and assessment and fail to impartially discern the authentic distinction of things. In order to discover and identify the nature of the intrinsic existence, it is important to remain susceptible because the phenomenon itself must be distinguished for what it actually is and not as we presume it to be.

Within the distinction between perception and immediate cognition lies the origin of human misconception concerning ourselves and the phenomenal world. Upon apparent knowledge, we fabricate an interpretation and explanation of existence that prejudices our view through prior appraisal and exposition. We fail to engage phenomena directly because our approach is strongly compromised by accumulated discrimination.

The more erudite and considerable our acumen, the greater the difficulty to restrain our conjecture and expectations. The methodical analyst and researcher imagines that through a systematic approach and by subsequent, stringent testing, an objective and decisive outcome is certain. But physical research is only applicable to material conditions and they alone do not comprise the fullness.

It is impossible to arrive at conclusive knowledge merely through an examination of partial evidence. The physical appearance is only the utmost extremity of a circumstance that in reality cannot exist separately from the intangible volume. Thus, if we are preoccupied merely with the physical conditions of things, we inevitably overlook the entirety and that omission presents us with an inexplicable conundrum. We find that our conclusions are disproportionate and discordant when applied to everyday, human experience. The scientific approach inherently concerns material conditions and, faced with an insolvable dilemma we regress to hypotheses and philosophical speculation that is inappropriately established upon purely physical research.

The extravagant approach of the mystic is equally disconcerting because the material status of phenomena is disregarded and an imaginative speculation prevail that is without sensible coordinates. This is as misleading as materialistic, Western philosophy because human intelligence cannot navigate within conditions that exist entirely without bearings. Consequently, all manner of fantasy and pretense masquerades as reality with absurd repercussions.

Furthermore, the human being is encumbered through a capricious disposition that augments and intensifies both the cumbersome perception of the materialist and the giddy impulsiveness of the cryptic occultist. Considerable difficulty arises through a disassociated emotionality that allures and arrests the affections. It is the passions and sentiments that must become assuaged and composed within the human heart otherwise we remain vulnerable to the dominance and whim of all manner of compulsions.

Unfortunately, we cannot remedy the disarray of our own psyche because, composed of discord it cannot self-ameliorate. The psychoanalyst and pharmacologist may present the stopgap expedient of insight and mood alteration but they do not offer a permanent transformation. Intervention must transpire within the depths of the heart itself where it is inaccessible to reason or medication.

The manner whereby the afflicted, human heart is restored, is through the confidential influence of immanent caritas. The human soul cannot alleviate itself, but it can open to the restorative expediency of sublime benevolence. Our part is openhearted sincerity and the experience of the mere presence of immanent caritas is itself curative.

When we permit ourselves to be cherished by sublime benevolence, we relinquish the pursuit of what we imagine is in our interest and permit the inauguration of a noble and generous disposition. We find that the new mentality is entirely differently established because it rests not upon dearth and inadequacy but upon quiet contentment.

27. Theory and Speculation

***Theory** is the fruit of reflection, it serves the purposes of science; practice will be incomplete when theory is false; **Speculation** belongs more to the imagination; it has therefore less to do with realities; it is that which is rarely to be reduced to practice, and can, therefore, seldomer be brought to the test of experience.*

Theory and speculation become prevalent when the conventional, cognitive approach reaches the extent of its application and relevancy. If we apply the criteria ideally adapted to physical research in an attempt to establish a philosophy that explains existence, then the resultant construct will be inevitably tendentious. In other words, the conclusions of a materially adapted investigation will remain of the same character as the particular methodology applied.

Physical properties are scrutinized through physically appropriate technology. Thereby we expand our knowledge concerning material circumstances. However, we run into difficulties when we endeavor to explore physically unamenable conditions and attempt to apply inappropriate means in the service of our researches into the intangible dimensions of material conditions. The qualitative dimension of something, for example, is elusive to exclusively physical investigation.

Thus, for practical convenience a color may be represented by a digital formula, but the actual phenomenon cannot be adequately represented in terms of wavelength frequency and photon strength because they are the properties of the effects of color and not the actual distinction. A numerical abstraction does not depict the intrinsic particularity of the phenomenon itself.

But specialized science, according to the particular approach, wrestles relentlessly endeavoring to construct an understanding of existence in terms of a selective, abstruse perspective. Where the scrutiny of the obvious conditions becomes insufficient and breaks down through the inadequacy of the frame of reference, incompatible circumstances are ingeniously reduced and quantified. An elaborate, hypothetical extension is constructed that is amenable to accepted scholarship whereby in order to achieve comprehension, we manufacture a tractable theory that appropriately corresponds to the conditions of our approach.

However, the consensus of a scientific collegiate does not certify the authenticity of an accepted ideology; it merely signifies agreement within a similar, entirely materialistic mentality. Inevitably, materialistic, Western philosophy is exclusively concerned with the superficial conditions of things because essential significances that reveal the authentic distinction of phenomena are irreconcilable with a shallow, temporal perspective.

Agnosticism is worn as a badge of honor that conceals a fundamental antipathy and lethargy towards nonmaterial conditions even though the physically elusive significance of things is commonly recognizable and universally experienced. In this sense, we observe that we are subjected to a humanly detrimental, contrived philosophy that is willfully partisan. It is established upon belief and conviction and not through the discipline of science. It is a persuasion, alike to any other position that must be intellectually substantiated in order to be convincing because it is otherwise not straightforwardly evident.

If the materialistic academician were to explore the intangible significance of things, it would be essential to develop the practice of immediate cognition because essential existence in unamenable to physical scrutiny. Otherwise, circumstances can be only subjectively assessed and the research will consequently remain inconclusive. Exploration of immediate cognitions requires a significant degree of open-mindedness that poses a challenge to established scholarship because human, incorporeal singularity is an unacceptable concept to the materialistically preoccupied mentality. Thus, the way forward is obscured through an entrenched, temporally established philosophy.

It is easy to evaluate existence merely upon the strength of the most obvious circumstances and it is easy to ignore information that is incompatible with physicism. There is no anticipation of progress towards greater, human autonomy in materialistic philosophy because the weighty questions concerning human, temporal existence remain unaddressed. We merely indulge an increasingly entrenched, materialistic superficiality, void of realistic connotation.

But from the perspective of human advancement the overlooked, intangible measure of material conditions is extremely significant because pertinence resides within the character, caliber and distinction of things and not merely in the carapace. A materialistically established philosophy will always appear impoverished and barren because if it excludes the intrinsic significance of things, that which remains is merely the inconsequential hollow.

28. The Essential View

***Criterion**...signifies the mark or rule by which one may judge. The criterion is employed only in matters of judgment; the **Standard** is used in the ordinary concerns of life. The former serves for determining the characters and qualities of things; the latter for defining quantity and measure.*

The efficacy of immediate cognition cannot be determined through intellectual brilliance or philosophical rationalization. The effectiveness of direct engagement rests upon the viewpoint of the human, essential distinction and, consequently, it is the ipseity itself and not the rational faculties that ascertain legitimacy and significance.

The denial of the reality of emphatic, incorporeal individuality, impedes the discovery of essential wisdom because it is only the human, intrinsic distinction that is able to recognize the essential condition of things. If its existence is denied and it is supposed that the body alone is the exclusive, human identity, then immediate cognition will remain merely a conceptual proposition and nothing more, while our perception will continue to be cursory.

The essential ipseity discovers its own uniqueness and repositions itself as the sovereign distinction of the human constitution. From the perspective of our essential existence, we discover the quintessential merit of everything else. Against the light of elemental existence, the isolated, material circumstances that are thought to possess the entire significance of phenomena, appear superficial because they merely represent the outer shell and of themselves they lack consequence.

Thus, it is foregone to anticipate that someone who denies the existence of their own incorporeal, intrinsic distinction, will find themselves to be constitutionally unable to conclusively evaluate the merit of immediate cognition. They will be categorically inhibited from experiencing direct discernment for themselves because they deny the existence of the crucial agency of their own essential viewpoint.

Furthermore, the conventional cognitive faculties of deductive rationale and analytical investigation can only estimate the existence of something that must be directly engaged in order to be recognized. However, it is pointless to argue against the entrenched position of the materialist because the two approaches of intellective evaluation as opposed to immediate cognition are entirely incommensurate. The materialist will assume that intelligence derived through immediate cognition, is the result of subjective experience and will thereupon hold it in question.

The importance of the human ipseity remains conceptually abstract without the incidence of direct engagement. Thus, the intense objectivity of immediate cognition, that takes places without intermediary evaluation, will be incomprehensible because its significance is physically elusive and consequently imperceptible to an exclusively materialistic perspective.

The existence of something that cannot be physically corroborated will elude scientific methodology even though its acquaintance may be familiar through common experience. Without the inmost pertinence as an extension of the obvious, material conditions, our perception inevitably lacks penetration and relevance. However, the intangible volume of phenomena and the intrinsic distinction of the individual, are far more significant than the temporal, physical appearance because they possess meaningfulness through their elemental status.

The intangible merit of a phenomenon is its qualitative value and intrinsic distinction or, in the case of organization, the conceptual origin. The authentic identification of something and of ourselves does not consist of the material constitution but of the content. The physical appearance is the consequence of the intrinsic connotation and the particular, qualitative manner of its existence.

We assume that the appearance is the epitome of a phenomena whereas, in reality, the origin and impetus, while physically imperceptible, is vastly consequential. Hence, we reduce, analyze and scrutinize the structure and constitution of things imagining that we will discover the quiddity within the detail but our subsequent findings are barren of meaning and value. Thereby, the significance of the entirety as a statement of existence is overlooked and the meaningful volume that anticipates the physical representation, remains obscure. Since the connotation exists intangibly and essentially, and is imperceptible from an exclusively physical viewpoint.

If there were no human, intangible distinction, the proposition of immediate cognition would be meaningless. It is the existence of the essential ipseity that makes direct engagement possible and leads to the recognition of our emphatic existence. Our intrinsic integrity, in a similar manner to all phenomena, exists intangibly and elementally. Thus, we are inherently endowed with the capacity to recognize the fundamental status of existence of ourselves, one another and of all other things.

29. Caprice

__Fanciful__ is said of that which is irregular in the taste or judgment; __Fantastical__ is said of that which violates all propriety as well as regularity; the former may consist of a simple deviation from the rule; the latter is something extravagant.

A perspective towards existence that positions the physical conditions of things above their essential significance, will inevitably fashion a philosophy that is correspondingly desultory and aimless. Hence, materialistic, Western philosophy rests upon the assumption of capricious but fortuitous influences acting randomly against conveniently positioned circumstances. This is the inevitable outcome of an over-exaggeration of the material status and properties of things at the expense of essential substance. Consequently, it is as barren of consequence as the shallow nature of the information upon which it is established.

It must occur at some level, to those who promote a simplistic, philosophical explanation of existence that is established exclusively upon physically derived evidence, that something of significance has been overlooked. A brief exchange with the staunch materialist reveals two interesting considerations. The one concerns an essential contradiction between philosophy and experience while the other standpoint suggests an antipathy for anything that might even indirectly advance a religious precept.

Thus, the clichéd retort to challenge is that if a particular position implies the existence of intangible conditions, it necessarily contravenes established science. Furthermore, only tangible circumstances are considered objectively verifiable. All other states are treated as if of lesser merit because they are thought to be only subjectively determined which makes them uncertain from the perspective of mensuration. Therefore, we chose readily verifiable, physical assets as the certain basis of an understanding of existence and conveniently ignore the intangible merit of things.

Science is the watchword of the materialist even though the conclusions of Materialistic, Western philosophy concerning the nature of life remain hypothetical because they cannot be empirically demonstrated as conclusive. Inevitably, the intangible quality, value or distinction of something that we consistently experience, contradicts the exclusively physical disassociation.

Science is used as a comprehensive panacea that conceals its misuse in the province of philosophy. An ideology may be implied by certain physical circumstances but if it cannot be conclusively demonstrated as extant, it remains merely speculative. If we discover and subsequently apply the mechanical principles and technical attributes of things, it does not follow that existence is exclusively physical. It merely shows that if we isolate the tangible proportion of things and extrapolate our technical comprehension to encompass the entirety of existence, we will inevitably contrive a worldview that is materialistically accentuated.

The conclusions and confident pronouncements of materialistic science inevitably reveal an extraordinarily bleak and indiscriminate depiction of life. This is because it is a process of inquiry particularly suited to the investigation of physical conditions. Consequently, it is entirely inappropriate in terms of philosophy because it is selective in its application and not comprehensively relevant. The tangible aspects and properties of things are exhaustively investigated and upon that sole basis we imagine that we can successfully evaluate existence. Thus, we construct a physical delineation as if the entirety were represented through the material conditions.

      The ensuing summary of life in merely technical terms inevitably has a devastating impact upon the human psyche because it merely represent the blatant, superficial characteristics of things and encompasses and defines humanity in similarly corporeal terms. Subsequently, culture disintegrates because materialistic philosophy will have us believe that existence is hopeless and inane, and we find that we cannot repudiate that viewpoint without resort to subjectively derived, counter-information. Thus, despondent, the human being pursues merely temporal gratification rather than cultivation and refinement because the temporal, material perspective towards existence is obviously convincing and seems beyond reproach.

      A vague and ambiguous religious or uncertain mystical interpretation is scarcely an improvement but merely presents a polar opposite perspective. Between the doctrinal architects and ecclesiastical hierarchy, one is often impressed with an acute sense of essential ignorance concealed by a deference for a narrow dogmatism.

      Thus, there appears on the surface to be limited

respite or reprieve. But the recognition of the essential falsity of materialistic, Western philosophy and an understanding of how through misapplication it came to define all of existence, inevitably promises optimism.

Simply put, the limited reach of scientific specialization towards areas beyond its compass presents a misconstrued philosophy that is remote from reality. In every sense, the viewpoint of a physically exclusive philosophy will be inevitably shallow and superficially established because it overlooks the essential significance of things. Furthermore, materialism contradicts commonplace, human experience.

30. Caritas

***Synchronous, Simultaneous, Contemporaneous** all mean occurring at the same time. Simultaneous...means occurring at exactly the same instant. Synchronous...means happening within the same period of time, but not necessarily at exactly the same instant. Contemporaneous...means living or happening within the same period, the period being thought of not merely as a division of time, as in the case of synchronous, but as an age, a generation, a period marked by certain characteristics distinguishing it from other period.*

Maintaining a determined constancy towards immanent caritas through openhearted sincerity and susceptibility, must become the urgent, human occupation of this time because we are witnessing a rampant, further regression towards self-absorption instead of maturity and emancipation. Thereby the potential of human, sovereign autonomy and existential liberty is deferred and, meanwhile, further ethical decline is inevitable.

We cannot progress and simultaneously maintain a self-circumscribed disposition. But our task is not soul-searching analysis and the endless investigation and scrutiny of our every thought and motive. This only leads to further confusion because the root cause of our disquiet remains intact. We cannot auto-ameliorate self-circumscription. Our attempts to do lead to self-righteousness and Puritanism, and the duplicity of seeming to make progress.

Similarly, striving for bliss through arcane, esoteric disciplines and self-imposed abnegation that attempts to attain liberty without essential maturation, fails to address the origin of human, arrested evolution. The individual works, as it were, from the outside in and strives thereby to circumvent mortal existence through mysticism and hopes thereby to escape.

Into the former category must also fall the expectation that if certain formulaic practices and rituals are performed, advantageous ramifications will ensue. Fascination with the miraculous is common even within the most conventional religions and not merely the domain of voodooism and the like. But it distracts from human, essential maturation through digression in much the same way that an anthropomorphic misinterpretation of the concept of maturation likewise tarnishes the central dynamic of human progression through mystery and dogma. Consequently, the agnostic despises and reviles the entirety as presumptuous and overlooks the central significance.

Human will is required not towards the achievement of a transformation, but in making the heart receptive to conditions that are already established and individually accessible in readiness for our expedient application. Constancy and receptivity of heart towards immanent caritas, inevitably inaugurates within the human soul, the establishment of an alternative, paradigmatic constitution.

A restructured complexion that is without egocentricity, emancipates the individual and presages the institution of the human, essential ipseity as the authentic identification. From the viewpoint of the essential, individual identity, all things are apprehended in their elemental condition. We are no longer preoccupied merely with the superficial periphery of things but engage the full volume of existence wherein lies meaningfulness and consequence.

A revolutionary, new archetype of soul is ready for our acceptance and adoption. But it is beyond human ability to achieve this essential transformation because we have no concept of its expression. Thus, we set aside what we imagine we know concerning human maturity and emancipation while dismissing the accumulated canon of religious and esoteric dogma. Thereby our approach is straightforward and unaffected. Through openhearted sincerity, an exhaustive reconstitution of soul is initiated through the benevolence of immanent caritas.

Other Books by the Same Author

TOWARDS A MEANINGFUL FUTURE
The Continuum of the Qualitative Expansion of the Soul

THE IMMANENT PRINCIPLE OF INTEGRITY AND GOODWILL
The Integration of the Principle of Virtue within the Human heart

THE EVOLUTIONARY IMPERATIVE OF OUR TIME
The Crucial Establishment of an Inspired Ethos with the Individual, Human Heart, appropriate to a Meaningful Future

RECONCILIATION WITH HUMAN DESTINY
The Surrender of the Heart-of-the-Soul as the Expedient Approach Towards Direct Engagement with the Immanent Exemplar of a Future, Human Disposition

THE QUALITATIVE EVOLUTION OF THE SOUL
The Evolutionary Transformation of the Human Soul Through Openhearted Sincerity Towards Immanent Caritas

THE SUPERNAL ETHOS
Unanimity with the Divine Nature

THE BEGINNING OF WISDOM
Knowledge through Immediate Engagement

UNDER THE AEGIS OF IMMANENT CARITAS
The Reorientation of the Human, Disparate Self-circumscribed Mentality

THE DECEPTION OF MATERIALISTIC WESTERN PHILOSOPHY
An Exploration of the Physically Elusive Volume of Existence

THE MEANINGFUL VOLUME OF EXISTENCE
An Exploration of the Overlooked Intangible Significance of Phenomena

THE OBSOLETE SELF
Individual Uniqueness and Significance beyond Egocentrism

HUMAN SOVEREIGN AUTONOMY
The Discovery of the Human Ipseity and its Establishment as the Essential Authority of the Human Constitution

THE TRANSFORMATION OF THE SOUL
From Self-centeredness to Sovereign Autonomy

THE IMPLICATION OF HUMAN, INCORPOREAL EXISTENCE
The Overlooked Significance of the Intangible and Qualitative Dimension of Existence

IMMEDIATE EXPERIENTIAL COGNITION
The Inherent Human Capacity of Immediate Engagement

www.ingramcontent.com/pod-product-compliance
Lightning Source LLC
Chambersburg PA
CBHW070809100426
42742CB00012B/2314